W9-BPJ-389

The Vietnam War

Other titles in the World History Series

The Age of Colonialism
Ancient Egypt
Ancient Greece
Apartheid in South Africa
The Byzantine Empire
The Early Middle Ages
Elizabethan England
The Late Middle Ages
The Nuremberg Trials
Religion and World Conflict
The Relocation of the North American Indian
The Roman Empire
The Roman Republic
World War I

The Vietnam War

Hal Marcovitz

LUCENT BOOKS

An imprint of Thomson Gale, a part of The Thomson Corporation

Detroit • New York • San Francisco • New Haven, Conn. • Waterville, Maine • London

LIBRARY OF CONGRESS CATALOGING-IN-PUBLICATION DATA

Marcovitz, Hal.
   Vietnam War / by Hal Marcovitz.
      p. cm. — (World history series)
   Includes bibliographical references and index.
   ISBN-13: 978-1-4205-0024-0 (hardcover)
   1. Vietnam War, 1961–1975. I. Title.
   DS557.7.M356 2007
   959.704'3—dc22

                                                    2007025989

ISBN-10: 1-4205-0024-4
Printed in the United States of America

Contents

Foreword   6
Important Dates at the Time of the Vietnam War   8

Introduction:
The Vietnam War   10

Chapter One:
Elusive Independence   13

Chapter Two:
Escalation   27

Chapter Three:
Struggle in the United States   40

Chapter Four:
"Peace Is at Hand"   55

Chapter Five:
The Failure of Vietnamization   68

Chapter Six:
After the Vietnam War   80

Notes   93
For Further Reading   96
Index   98
Picture Credits   103
About the Author   104

Foreword

Each year, on the first day of school, nearly every history teacher faces the task of explaining why his or her students should study history. Many reasons have been given. One is that lessons exist in the past from which contemporary society can benefit and learn. Another is that exploration of the past allows us to see the origins of our customs, ideas, and institutions. Concepts such as democracy, ethnic conflict, or even things as trivial as fashion or mores, have historical roots.

Reasons such as these impress few students, however. If anything, these explanations seem remote and dull to young minds. Yet history is anything but dull. And therein lies what is perhaps the most compelling reason for studying history: History is filled with great stories. The classic themes of literature and drama—love and sacrifice, hatred and revenge, injustice and betrayal, adversity and overcoming adversity—fill the pages of history books, feeding the imagination as well as any of the great works of fiction do.

The story of the Children's Crusade, for example, is one of the most tragic in history. In 1212 Crusader fever hit Europe. A call went out from the pope that all good Christians should journey to Jerusalem to drive out the hated Muslims and return the city to Christian control. Heeding the call, thousands of children made the journey. Parents bravely allowed many children to go, and entire communities were inspired by the faith of these small Crusaders. Unfortunately, many boarded ships were captained by slave traders, who enthusiastically sold the children into slavery as soon as they arrived at their destination. Thousands died from disease, exposure, and starvation on the long march across Europe to the Mediterranean Sea. Others perished at sea.

Another story, from a modern and more familiar place, offers a soul-wrenching view of personal humiliation but also the ability to rise above it. Hatsuye Egami was one of 110,000 Japanese Americans sent to internment camps during World War II. "Since yesterday we Japanese have ceased to be human beings," he wrote in his diary. "We are numbers. We are no longer Egamis, but the number 23324. A tag with that number is on every trunk, suitcase and bag. Tags, also, on our breasts." Despite such dehumanizing treatment, most internees worked hard to control their bitterness. They created workable communities inside the camps and demonstrated again and again their loyalty as Americans.

These are but two of the many stories from history that can be found in the pages of the Lucent Books World History series. All World History titles rely on sound research and verifiable evidence, and all give students a clear sense of time, place, and chronology through maps and timelines as well as text.

All titles include a wide range of authoritative perspectives that demonstrate the complexity of historical interpretation and sharpen the reader's critical thinking skills. Formally documented quotations and annotated bibliographies enable students to locate and evaluate sources, often instantaneously via the Internet, and serve as valuable tools for further research and debate.

Finally, Lucent's World History titles present rousing good stories, featuring vivid primary source quotations drawn from unique, sometimes obscure sources such as diaries, public records, and contemporary chronicles. In this way, the voices of participants and witnesses as well as important biographers and historians bring the study of history to life. As we are caught up in the lives of others, we are reminded that we too are characters in the ongoing human saga, and we are better prepared for our own roles.

1858
Armada of French warships arrives in Da Nang, a port city of Vietnam, launching a century-long occupation of Vietnam by the French military.

1861
First shots in the U.S. Civil War are fired at Fort Sumter in South Carolina.

1945
First electronic computer, ENIAC, goes into operation at the University of Pennsylvania in Philadelphia.

1963
Betty Friedan publishes *The Feminine Mystique*, sparking the women's liberation movement in the United States.

1953
Viet Minh defeat French at Battle of Dien Bien Phu; Geneva peace conference splits Vietnam into two countries.

1860   1940   1945   1950   1955   1960   1965

1941
Japanese attack Pearl Harbor; Ho Chi Minh, a Communist, establishes the Viet Minh to fight against the Japanese and Vichy French for Vietnamese independence.

1952
Elizabeth II becomes queen of England.

1964
Congress passes Gulf of Tonkin Resolution after North Vietnamese gunboats fire on a U.S. Navy ship; the Vietnam War, or Second Indochina War, commences.

1946
First Indochina War commences; Viet Minh battle French occupiers in war for independence.

Time of the Vietnam War

1968
Tet Offensive; Communist forces suffer major defeat, but the battle convinces U.S. political leaders to find a way to withdraw American troops.

1979
Genocidal Khmer Rouge regime in Cambodia is ousted by Vietnamese troops.

1993
U.S. president Bill Clinton eases economic sanctions on Vietnam, permitting U.S. companies to do business in the Communist nation.

2007
Vietnamese prime minister Nguyen Tan Dung conducts an online chat with the Vietnamese people and discloses that his son attends college in the United States.

1991
Communist regime collapses in the Soviet Union.

1970   1975   1980   1985   1990   1995   2000   2005

1975
South Vietnam falls to the Communists.

2001
The United States invades Afghanistan after Islamic terrorists attack the World Trade Center in New York and the Pentagon in Washington, D.C.

1973
Cease-fire declared in Vietnam War; all U.S. troops withdraw from Southeast Asia.

2003
American troops invade Iraq and oust dictator Saddam Hussein.

1969
First astronauts walk on the moon.

The Vietnam War

The Vietnam War was a devastating conflict that left deep scars on all of the countries involved. Approximately 2 million Vietnamese—an estimated 10 percent of the country's population—were killed or wounded during the war, with another 1 million becoming refugees. Bombs and chemical warfare took a substantial toll on the country's infrastructure and land. The war cost nearly sixty thousand American lives, helped bring down two presidential administrations, and led to widespread public dissent in the United States. The painful lessons learned during the Vietnam War continue to affect American foreign policy today.

The Superpowers

The Vietnam War must be considered within the context of a larger conflict that occurred during the second half of the twentieth century: the Cold War. The Cold War was not an actual military confrontation but a term used to describe a period of icy relations and intense competition involving the United States, the Soviet Union, and their various allies. Although the United States had been allied with the Soviet Union during World War II (1939–1945), soon after that conflict ended the two superpowers found themselves competing against one another for influence over dozens of nations in Europe, Asia, Africa, and South America.

After 1945 American foreign policy increasingly focused on stopping the spread of communism, the ideological basis of the Soviet form of government, into other countries. In places as diverse as Turkey, Greece, Guatemala, Taiwan, and Indonesia, American political leaders were able to thwart Communist movements by propping up shaky democracies or backing outright dictatorships led by strongmen who opposed the Soviet Union. In other places Communists succeeded in gaining power. One of these places was China, where the Communist regime of Mao Tse-tung took power in 1949 following a civil war against the U.S.-supported nationalist forces of Chiang Kai-shek. The Chinese Communists would become players in the Cold War, serving as occasional but wary allies of the Soviets.

For more than forty years, until the collapse of the Soviet Union in 1991, the Cold War would affect life in virtually every nation on the planet. For the most part it was characterized by the political and military tensions between the superpowers, as both countries built up enormous arsenals of thermonuclear warheads as well as stocks of more conventional weapons. Occasionally, the Cold War intensified. In 1950, for example, Communist North Korea's army—equipped with weapons provided by China—invaded South Korea. A United Nations force led by the Americans quickly mobilized and repulsed the offensive. For three years the two sides fought to a standstill. Finally, a cease-fire was called, and an uneasy peace has remained in place to this day.

Beginning in the 1950s American leaders based their foreign policy decisions on the so-called domino theory—a belief that when one country fell under the control of the Communists, neighboring countries were likely to become Communist as well, just as dominoes in a line will knock each other over. President Lyndon B. Johnson invoked the domino theory in his explanation of why the United States needed to fight in Vietnam. "If this little nation goes down the drain and can't maintain her independence, ask yourself what is going to happen to all the other little nations," he said. "So somebody must stand there and try to help the little nations protect themselves from the nations who would provoke aggression."[1]

Due to the tide of Cold War politics, Vietnam became one of the hotspots in America's fight against communism.

The Situation in Vietnam

The Vietnam War pitted governments in North and South Vietnam fighting for control over the country in a conflict fueled by the Cold War players. In northern Vietnam a popular Communist government backed by the Soviets and Chinese held control; the Soviets and Chinese supplied arms, money, and military advisers to the North with the aim of adding another Communist country to their sphere of influence. In southern Vietnam a weak and corrupt government propped up by American money and diplomacy wielded power. The Americans and a handful of allies provided arms, money, and troops to the South in a campaign to maintain a noncommunist nation in what they regarded as one of the most strategic areas of the planet. Townsend Hoopes, a former U.S. undersecretary of the air force and author of several books and essays on Vietnam, explains the reason for American involvement in Southeast Asia:

> Every American policy in Vietnam . . . ranging from economic aid to military training to military supply to sending of advisors, continued to be based on what seemed a self-evident proposition: namely, that the expansion of "International Communism" presented everywhere, and in nearly every form, a direct menace to U.S. security that had to be stopped—in the last resort by whatever means necessary.[2]

To prevent Vietnamese Communists from taking control of the country, American political leaders used the military resources of the United States. At first hundreds and then thousands of military advisers were dispatched to the country to train and guide the South Vietnamese army. Eventually, the United States would commit hundreds of thousands of its own troops as well as billions of dollars in military aid. But despite being the wealthiest country in the world, the United States was unable to achieve its aims in Vietnam, and the war ended in a humiliating defeat for the superpower.

Today, more than three decades after the end of the war, Vietnam remains governed by a Communist regime. However, the world has changed greatly in that time: The Soviet Union no longer exists, China has become a major trading partner with the United States, and international communism has ceased to be a threat to democracy. During the Vietnam War, few people would have predicted this scenario.

Chapter One

Elusive Independence

During Vietnam's long and tortured existence, various attempts have been made to gain independence for its people. In the first century, for instance, sisters Trung Trac and Trung Nhi led a rebellion against Chinese invaders. The uprising briefly brought independence, and the Trung sisters are revered as heroic figures in Vietnamese history.

Nearly two thousand years later, the Vietnamese people would again be led against invaders by a revolutionary figure. This leader was the charismatic and fierce nationalist Nguyen That Thanh, who was known by various names and eventually took the name Ho Chi Minh (which means "he who is enlightened").

French Invasion

Vietnam, a country of some 127,000 square miles (329,000 sq. km), borders the South China Sea in a region known as Indochina. For much of Vietnam's history, the country fell under the brutal rule of the Chinese, although there were occasional periods of independence. But even when independent, the Vietnamese hardly enjoyed peace. Civil wars were common, emperors who tried to unite the country were largely ineffective, and powerful clans and wealthy families often held the real power.

In the 1830s French Catholic missionaries arrived in Vietnam, and soon the French government sent soldiers to the country. Such imperialist activity was not uncommon, as the 1830s were part of an era of widespread colonial expansion by the European powers. Great Britain, France, Germany, Belgium, and other European nations sent their armies into Africa and Asia to open trade routes and stake claims to rich natural resources.

On August 31, 1858, a small French army arrived at the port city of Da Nang in Vietnam. There were twenty-five hundred french soldiers in an armada of fourteen warships. The Vietnamese resisted the French, and the French also struggled because they were ill prepared for the climate and conditions they found in the hot and marshy country. Hundreds of French soldiers died from guerilla attacks in the jungle or from disease. Still, by 1859 a second French invasion force had seized the southern city of Saigon, after which France claimed Vietnam as a colony. Soon the French moved into the neighboring countries of Laos and Cambodia as well.

Path to Liberation

The French remained in power for decades, even as much of their army and many of their resources were otherwise occupied defending native soil during World War I (1914–1918). At the conclusion of that war, the Allies (France, Great Britain, the United States, and others that had been on the same side during the war) met in Paris to negotiate the Treaty of Versailles. During the negotiations, Ho Chi Minh—who then was living in France and had become a leader of the Vietnamese expatriate community in that country—asked for admission to the peace conference to speak on behalf of Vietnamese independence. He was denied, and France remained in control of Vietnam.

Shortly after the peace conference, Ho helped found the French Communist Party. He had studied the writings of the Bolshevik leader Vladimir Lenin. (The Bolsheviks were radicals in the Russian

The Deer Mission

In July 1945 three American commandos parachuted into the mountains of North Vietnam and made their way to the camp of Ho Chi Minh and some two hundred ragged, ill-armed Viet Minh guerillas. The commandos' mission was to arm and train the guerillas and organize an assault on Japanese positions in Vietnam. By then the Nazi regime in Germany had fallen and the Allies were concentrating their forces for an all-out assault on Japan so World War II could end. In Vietnam the plan to attack the Japanese became known as the Deer Mission.

When the Americans arrived they found Ho emaciated and suffering from malaria, so the commandos provided food and medicine to the Communist leader, who recovered and regained his strength. However, before the Deer Mission could be launched, the atomic bombs that the United States dropped on Japan in early August 1945 brought World War II to an abrupt halt. For Ho's Viet Minh guerillas, this brief training period would mark the last time they fought alongside American soldiers.

Socialist Party who formed the Communist Party in 1918 in Russia.) Lenin called on oppressed peoples of the world to fight off the European powers that had colonized their countries. "What emotion, enthusiasm and clear-sightedness, and confidence [Lenin] instilled in me!" Ho recalled years later. "Though sitting alone in my room, I shouted aloud as if addressing large crowds: 'Dear martyrs, compatriots! This is what we need, this is what we need, this is the path of our liberation.'"[3]

In 1940 the armies of Nazi Germany conquered France, and the puppet Vichy government was installed to administer French territories. Secretly, however, Germany turned Vietnam over to Japan, Germany's ally in Asia. The Vichy French continued officially to administer Vietnam, but the Japanese held the real power in the country.

By then Ho had returned to Southeast Asia and formed the Viet Minh, a nationalist group whose aim was to unify the country under a Vietnamese government. Ho had organized the Viet Minh in 1941 in a cave near the remote village of Pac Bo, where he and his followers hid from the Japanese. It was a humble beginning, but Ho had grand plans for the future of his country.

"The hour has struck!" Ho declared in the Viet Minh's first message to the Vietnamese people. "Raise aloft the insurrectionary banner and guide the people throughout the country to overthrow the Japanese and the French! The sacred call of the fatherland is resounding in your ears: the blood of our heroic predecessors who sacrificed their lives is stirring in your hearts! Let us rise up quickly! Victory to Vietnam's Revolution!"[4]

August Revolution

The Viet Minh soon became a popular force among the Vietnamese. The French and Japanese had maintained a brutal occupation of the country; during World War II, when famine hit Vietnam, the Japanese and French confiscated food for their own troops while the Japanese also shipped food back to Japan, which was having its own problems feeding its people. To help the Vietnamese, Ho's Viet Minh guerillas raided food warehouses and distributed rice and grain to the peasants. To the Vietnamese, Ho became known as "Uncle Ho"—a benevolent and caring patriarch who would lead them out of oppression. Still, some 2 million Vietnamese peasants died in the famine.

Armed mostly with spears and machetes, the Viet Minh guerillas waged a jungle fight against the Japanese. Late in the war, the United States sent commandos into Vietnam to arm and train the Viet Minh guerillas, while Ho provided his new allies with intelligence on Japanese troop movements. As the Americans prepared the Vietnamese for an assault on Japanese positions, the Japanese withdrew from the country.

Ho called for Vietnam's independence as well as a total reorganization of the nation and its economy. Under Ho's plan, land and property would be seized from the wealthy Vietnamese who had collaborated with the French, and the land would be redistributed to the peasants.

Ho Chi Minh (second from left) stands beside other world Communist leaders at Lenin's mausoleum in Moscow. Lenin's writings would inspire Ho to unite Vietnam under communism.

Those ideas followed decidedly Communist principles.

Yet the Vietnamese were not left alone to follow Ho's plan or any other. Instead, the Chinese sent troops into the northern part of Vietnam while the British landed troops in southern Vietnam to administer the country until other arrangements could be decided upon. Again, Ho made a plea for independence—this time to the new American president, Harry Truman. Again, Ho was ignored. Meanwhile, in the South, the British rearmed the French, who began fighting against the Viet Minh forces.

In August 1945, just days after the atomic bombs fell on Japan, Ho and the Viet Minh marched into the capital, Hanoi, and declared themselves the rightful rulers of Vietnam. Ho called this declaration the "August Revolution." On September 2, 1945, some four hundred thousand Vietnamese citizens gathered in Ba Dinh Square in Hanoi. Ho declared the day Vietnam's Independence Day, and he spoke to the people as the self-proclaimed leader of a new country—the Democratic Republic of Vietnam.

Opposing Foreign Control

Ho's nationalist government did not last long in power. Soon some two hundred thousand Chinese troops moved into the North and took control. These were not

Communist Chinese troops; the anticommunist Chinese Nationalists, under U.S. ally Chiang Kai-shek, were still in power in China. At the Potsdam Conference late in World War II, the Allied powers had agreed that Chiang's army would oversee the disarming of Japanese forces in Vietnam.

Early in 1946 Ho entered talks with the French government. He did not want French officials back in control of his country, but he desperately wanted to be rid of the Chinese because historically that country had dominated Vietnam. Ho negotiated an agreement wherein administration of Vietnam was handed to France, which in turn agreed to recognize Vietnam as a free state within the French Union, a political entity created after World War II to include France and many of its colonies and territories. Negotiations were to commence immediately on turning the country over to a popularly elected Vietnamese government. When the terms were announced, the Chinese, not willing to risk a war against France, withdrew their troops from Vietnam. In May Ho left for Paris, where he expected to negotiate the framework for the election that would declare Vietnam an independent republic.

It did not take long for the Communist leader to conclude that the French had no intentions of withdrawing from Vietnam. Upon arriving in Paris the Vietnamese negotiators learned that only North Vietnam was to be free. French leaders regarded South Vietnam as a separate country, which they called Cochin China, a name they drew from the city of Kochi in southern India. The negotiations dragged on throughout the summer of 1946. Ho insisted that the South and North be unified into a single nation, but the French would not budge from their position. Vietnamese negotiator Pham Van Dong later recalled that the French displayed contempt for the Vietnamese and made brazen threats. "When the meeting began," according to Pham, "the chief of the French delegation, Max Andre, said to me, 'We only need an ordinary police operation for eight days to clean all of you out.' There was no need for negotiations."[5]

In the fall of 1946 Ho returned to Hanoi with no agreement in hand. And while the nationalist leader had been conducting the futile negotiations, sporadic fighting had broken out between Viet Minh guerillas and French troops. That November French troops shelled Haiphong, a harbor city that was a hotbed of Viet Minh resistance. Some six thousand Vietnamese died in the attack. The French next turned their attention to Hanoi, where they drove the Viet Minh, including Ho, into the mountains surrounding the city. On December 19, believing he had no other choice, Ho declared war on France.

War for Independence

The French enjoyed a clear military advantage as the conflict that became known as the First Indochina War commenced. The Viet Minh were poorly armed, while the French had modern weapons, mostly supplied by the United States, which feared a Communist takeover of Vietnam. But the Viet Minh guerillas had widespread support among the peasants. Nguyen Thi Dinh, a woman from the South, said:

At first we did not have any weapons except for bamboo spears. But in the northern part of our country, they were producing arms. I was appointed to go there to report on the situation in the South. Uncle Ho told me that he carried the South in the depth of his heart, and I should tell him what we needed so that the central government could supply us to fight the French and drive them out of the country. I replied that we needed guns. Uncle Ho said that the central government could only give us so many guns because they did not have many. The main thing, he said, was to capture the enemy's guns and use these guns against them.[6]

As the Viet Minh struggled to find weapons for its soldiers, French leaders installed a puppet government in Hanoi. In 1948 the former Vietnamese emperor, Bao Dai, was appointed as ruler.

In 1949 the Communist Chinese under Mao Tse-tung defeated Chiang Kai-shek's nationalist Chinese in a civil war, driving the nationalists from mainland China to the island of Taiwan. The most populous country in the world was now controlled by a Communist regime. A year later Mao's government started supplying the Viet Minh with guns and military advisers. Once armed by the Communist Chinese, the Viet Minh became a much more formidable opponent. In addition, Mao

extended diplomatic recognition to Ho's government, making China the first foreign power to recognize Ho Chi Minh as leader of the Vietnamese people. The Soviet Union soon extended diplomatic recognition to Ho as well. In response the United States, which was already helping to finance France's costly war against the Viet Minh, believed it had no alternative but to recognize Bao Dai's regime as the legitimate government of Vietnam.

In 1950 the Cold War turned hot when North Korean troops armed with Chinese weapons invaded South Korea. The United States took the lead in mobilizing an international military force to repel the attack, because American diplomats feared that China aimed to spread communism throughout Asia. Dean Rusk, a U.S. diplomat who would serve as secretary of state from 1961 to 1969, later explained: "It was decided on the very weekend of the North Korean attack that we would step up our aid very significantly to the French and to Southeast Asia. Because we did not know at that point whether or not the Chinese might attempt to move into that area as part of a general offensive in Asia."[7]

U.S. financial assistance in support of the French effort against the Communists in Vietnam increased, and by 1954 the United States had spent more than $1 billion a year on the war. Despite this substantial aid the French scored few military successes. After capturing a rural village or an urban neighborhood in Hanoi, French officials would declare the area pacified, but within weeks guerillas would return and take control back from

In an attempt to maintain its power over Vietnam, the French installed a puppet government in Hanoi, headed by Bao Dai (pictured).

the French occupiers. The climactic battle of the First Indochina War occurred at Dien Bien Phu in northwestern Vietnam, where, after a two-month siege, a Viet Minh force crushed a French army in May 1954.

Compromise in Geneva

On May 8, 1954, a day after the fall of Dien Bien Phu to the North Vietnamese, a conference was convened in Geneva, Switzerland, to work out a peace agreement. Vietnam was granted its independence along

Tactics at Dien Bien Phu

During the siege of Dien Bien Phu, Viet Minh soldiers dug miles of trenches and tunnels around the French positions, creating a network of hiding places from which they could launch assaults on the enemy. In *Vietnam: A History*, Stanley Karnow quotes Viet Minh colonel Bui Tin as recalling: "The shovel became our most important weapon. Everyone dug tunnels and trenches under fire, sometimes hitting hard soil and only advancing five or six yards a day. But we gradually surrounded Dienbeinphu with an underground network several hundred miles long, and we could tighten the noose around the French."

Meanwhile, the Viet Minh hauled heavy cannons high into the mountains—a feat French military leaders had thought impossible. Karnow quoted one French officer, Colonel Charles Piroth, who boasted, "No Viet Minh cannon will be able to fire three rounds before being destroyed by my artillery." Nevertheless, with artillery shells raining down from above and guerillas attacking from secret hiding places in the valley, it did not take long for the sixteen thousand French paratroopers trapped at Dien Bien Phu to succumb to the onslaught. Dien Bien Phu fell after just fifty-five days of fighting. As for Piroth, he committed suicide—two days after the first Viet Minh cannon shots were fired from their mountain outposts.

Quoted in Stanley Karnow, *Vietnam: A History*. New York: Penguin, 1997, p. 224.

with two other French colonies in Southeastern Asia, Laos and Cambodia. However, the compromise agreement called for Vietnam to be divided along the 17th parallel of latitude, temporarily creating two independent countries. The North would be turned over to Ho's Communists while the South would be administered by Bao Dai's regime. National elections intended to reunite the country were scheduled for 1956. The Soviets and Chinese, who sent diplomats to Geneva, urged Ho to accept the deal. Leaders of the two Communist powers feared the United States would intervene with troops if Ho attempted to take control of the entire country.

Ho grudgingly accepted the terms. He was confident that he enjoyed the support of the Vietnamese people and that the Communists would win the 1956 unification election. Ho returned to Hanoi, where he took power as head of the Democratic Republic of Vietnam, more familiarly known as North Vietnam. In the South, Bao Dai appointed the vehemently anticommunist politician Ngo Dinh Diem as the country's prime minister.

Under President Dwight D. Eisenhower, who had taken office in 1953, the United States continued to support anticommunist movements around the world. Beginning in 1954 America sent $100 million a year in aid to Diem's government in Saigon. In 1955 Diem held a referendum on the future of Bao Dai's monarchy, rigging the vote to ensure the outcome he wanted. Three days later he declared the South the Republic of Vietnam (better known as South Vietnam), with himself as president. That year the first American military advisers arrived in Saigon to help train the South Vietnamese army. With the Americans propping up the South Viet-

THE VIETNAM WAR

CHINA

NORTH
VIETNAM

Dien Bien Phu   Hanoi

LAOS   Gulf of
                             Tonkin

Vientiane

Mekong River

Demilitarized Zone (DMZ)

17th Parallel
Demarcation Line
(Geneva Accords, 1954)   Hue

                                          Da Nang

THAILAND

                                          My Lai

                                          South China
                                          Sea

CAMBODIA

Phnom
Penh   SOUTH
                       VIETNAM

                       Saigon

Gulf of
Thailand

0   150 miles

0   150 kilometers

namese government and the Soviets and Chinese giving support to Ho in the North, unification hardly seemed possible.

Strategic Hamlets

When Diem declared that the South would not participate in national elections, guerilla warfare erupted between the North and the South. Communists infiltrated Saigon, where they assassinated government officials and ambushed soldiers and police. In 1959 a secret supply line was cut through the jungle, linking North Vietnam and South Vietnam but also snaking through Cambodia and Laos. This supply line became known as the Ho Chi Minh Trail and would be used to ship arms to Communist guerillas in the South. A year later, an independent organization of Communist guerillas formed the National Liberation Front. Known more familiarly as the Vietcong, it became a close ally of the North in the years ahead.

Diem's regime was plagued by corruption, while Diem's brother Ngo Dinh Nhu, head of the secret police, used repressive and cold-blooded tactics to find Communist insurgents. Nhu's secret police searched rural villages, where they took young men suspected of guerilla activity away from their families. The police often tortured or murdered suspected members of the Vietcong. The Vietcong guerillas

At the Geneva Convention in 1954, Ho Chi Minh grudgingly agreed to divide Vietnam between north and south, setting the stage for a conflict that would rage for nearly two decades.

fought back. In addition to assassinating South Vietnamese officials, they won peasants over by promising them their own land and pledging to put an end to the abuses by Diem and Nhu.

In response Diem decided to isolate the peasants from the guerillas. He ordered the construction of thousands of fortified villages, known as strategic hamlets. Tens of thousands of peasants were herded into the villages, which were surrounded by moats and barbed-wire fences. Despite these precautions it did not take long for Vietcong guerillas to find ways to infiltrate the hamlets.

Public Burnings

By 1963 it was clear that Diem's regime was teetering on the edge of chaos. On May 8 an incident occurred in the city of Hue (pronounced *hWAY*) that led to the downfall of Diem. The event also made it abundantly clear to U.S. diplomats that unless they stepped in and stabilized the government, the South would fall to the Communists.

The event that made such an impact involved a group of Buddhist monks who gathered in Hue to celebrate a religious holiday. A low-level city official sent in police to break up the gathering. Word quickly spread through the Buddhist community, and within hours several thousand Buddhists gathered in front of a radio station to listen to a speech broadcast by one of their leaders. When police arrived at the radio station, they fired into the crowd, killing nine people.

Outraged, Buddhist leaders organized demonstrations throughout the country. Diem, a Catholic, shrugged off the protests, claiming they were staged by the Commu-

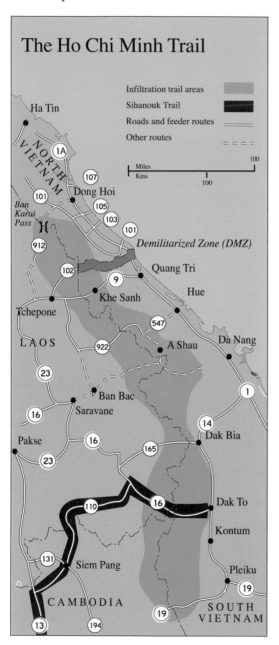

In order to better equip and arm guerilla warriors, the Vietcong cut a secret supply route through Vietnam, Cambodia, and Laos, known as the Ho Chi Minh Trail.

The Ho Chi Minh Trail

Infiltration trail areas
Sihanouk Trail
Roads and feeder routes
Other routes

Miles
Kms
100
100

Ha Tin

NORTH VIETNAM

1A

107

Dong Hoi

101

105

Ban Karai Pass

103

101

912

Demilitarized Zone (DMZ)

102

Quang Tri

9

Hue

Khe Sanh

Tchepone

547

LAOS

922

A Shau

Da Nang

23

Ban Bac

1

16

Saravane

Pakse

14

16

Dak Bia

23

165

Dak To

110

16

Kontum

131

Siem Pang

Pleiku

19

CAMBODIA

SOUTH VIETNAM

13

194

19

A group of monks and nuns sits on a Vietnamese road after their demonstration for religious freedom was stopped by South Vietnamese municipal and riot police.

nists. But instead of backing down, the Buddhists stepped up their protests and called for Diem's ouster. The demonstrators were often confronted by Nhu's agents, who roughed them up or hauled them away to jail.

On the morning of June 11 an elderly Buddhist monk sat down cross-legged in the middle of a busy Saigon intersection. Another monk doused him with gasoline and then set the elderly man on fire. News photographers captured the image of the burning Buddhist monk. The next day, the horrifying pictures were published on the front pages of newspapers all over the world.

Soon other Buddhists carried out similar demonstrations, vowing that still others would burn themselves unless Diem granted the Buddhists religious freedom. Convinced that the Communists had encouraged the suicidal burnings to destabilize his regime, Diem refused to yield.

Coup Against Diem

Diem had lost the support of his top military leaders, who started making plans to oust him. Officials in Washington also

Madame Nhu

The wife of South Vietnamese secret police leader Ngo Dinh Nhu was known to the world as Madame Nhu. Since her brother-in-law, South Vietnamese president Ngo Dinh Diem, was a bachelor, Madame Nhu served as the first lady of Vietnam during Diem's regime, from 1955 until his assassination in 1963.

Born Tran Le Xuan in 1924, Madame Nhu had a taste for Western fashion and style that helped alienate her brother-in-law from Vietnam's large Buddhist population. She also had an incendiary tongue and often publicly ridiculed enemies of the Diem regime.

In 1963, when the first Buddhist monk burned himself to death to call attention to Diem's repressive regime, Madame Nhu told an American television reporter: "What have the Buddhist leaders done comparatively? . . . The only thing they have done, they have barbecued one of their monks whom they have intoxicated . . . and even that barbecuing was done not even with self-sufficient means because they used imported gasoline."

Madame Nhu was on a visit to America in November 1963 when South Vietnamese military leaders staged a coup against Diem, murdering the president as well as her husband. The new regime barred her from returning. She is believed to be living in seclusion in the south of France.

Quoted in *American Experience*, PBS, "Vietnam Online." www.pbs.org/wgbh/amex/vietnam series/pt_02.html.

Madame Nhu, who served as South Vietnam's first lady during the Diem regime, gained the resentment of Buddist leaders and Vietnamese peasants for her sharp tongue and Western fashions.

decided that Diem had to go. By then the United States was spending more than $1 million a day to prop up Diem's government and provide guidance to the South Vietnamese army, which was in open warfare against the Vietcong. Some sixteen thousand American military advisers were in South Vietnam.

A cadre of South Vietnamese generals approached a U.S. Central Intelligence

Agency official, Lucien Conein, and asked for U.S. support in toppling Diem. Their request was forwarded to President John F. Kennedy, who decided that Diem should be given the opportunity to resign. In Saigon, U.S. ambassador Henry Cabot Lodge communicated the ultimatum to Diem, but the Vietnamese president refused to step down.

South Vietnamese military leaders felt they had to take action, so on November 1 their air force planes strafed the presidential residence in Saigon. Army troops searched the city for Diem and Nhu. They were found in a Catholic church, arrested, and quickly executed.

The Situation Grows Worse

After the collapse of Diem's regime, South Vietnam was governed by a shaky military regime that found itself unable to stabilize the nation. Seeing this weakness, the Vietcong grew bolder. In the countryside and in the streets of Saigon and other cities in the South, they stepped up attacks and assassinations of government officials—all with the support of Ho's government in the North.

In August 1964 three North Vietnamese gunboats patrolling the Gulf of Tonkin were alleged to have fired on a U.S. Navy destroyer, the *Maddox*. Two days later the *Maddox* and another destroyer, the *Turner*

Navy jets aboard the USS Constellation *prepare for flight during the Gulf of Tonkin incident in July 1963.*

Joy, reported that they were under a renewed attack. In Washington, D.C., President Lyndon B. Johnson, who had taken office after the assassination of Kennedy in November 1963, received the news. Although the president and his advisers were not certain about the nature of the incident—weeks later Johnson admitted to his secretary of defense that he doubted the second attack on the U.S. ships had actually occurred—they saw it as an opportunity for the United States to commit to a full military response against the Communist threat in Vietnam. At Johnson's urging, on August 7, 1964, the U.S. Congress passed the Gulf of Tonkin Resolution, granting Johnson power to use force in Southeast Asia. Although the resolution fell short of an actual declaration of war—in fact, war would never be officially declared—Johnson used its authority to justify sending American troops to fight on the side of South Vietnam. The Second Indochina War—known to Americans as the Vietnam War—had begun in earnest.

Chapter Two

Escalation

By the spring of 1965 the United States had begun an air force bombing campaign to destroy targets in North Vietnam and the first U.S. troops had landed in Vietnam. While the Americans and the South Vietnamese already had suffered some casualties before this campaign, American political leaders predicted that, in light of this onslaught of U.S. military might, it would not be long before Ho Chi Minh asked for peace.

But Ho did not ask for peace after all. In the North the Communists endured the bombing while they relied on the Soviet Union and China for supplies and arms, which they sent south along the Ho Chi Minh Trail to the Vietcong guerillas. Meanwhile, the American soldiers arriving in Vietnam found themselves engaging an enemy that was hard to find. As the Americans marched from village to village rooting out guerillas, they were forced to fight a relentless enemy skilled at striking quickly and then melting back

unseen into the thick jungle. Even though the United States would keep ratcheting up the pressure—by 1969 some 530,000 American troops were stationed in South Vietnam—the Americans always seemed to be a step behind.

Challenging the Americans

The first battle of the war took place before dawn on November 1, 1964, when one hundred Vietcong guerillas attacked an American air base at Bien Hoa, just north of Saigon. The guerillas completely surprised the American and South Vietnamese soldiers stationed at the base. The attack was launched from the jungle; the guerillas simply fired mortars and cannons into the base, then disappeared into the jungle before squads could be organized to search for them. As the sun rose, the Americans assessed the damage: six planes were destroyed and twenty others damaged. Five Americans and two South Vietnamese were killed, while more than one hundred sustained wounds.

More attacks would soon follow, and not only on military bases. On December 24, 1964, as a group of American officers gathered in the bar of the Brinks Hotel in downtown Saigon for a Christmas Eve party, a bomb suddenly exploded, killing two Americans and injuring fifty-eight others. Two Vietcong guerillas had set the bomb; they had been helped by a spy who had infiltrated the South Vietnamese government and knew the Americans would be gathering in the hotel that night.

The Vietcong staged another daring attack before dawn on February 7, 1965. They targeted an American army base at Pleiku, nearly 300 miles (483km) north of Saigon in a mountainous region known as the Central Highlands. Again, the Vietcong found the Americans sleeping and hurled shells into the camp from their jungle hideouts. This time eight Americans were killed, while another hundred suf-

A B-52 carpets the North Vietnamese landscape with bombs during Operation Rolling Thunder.

fered wounds. By staging such daring attacks, the Vietcong showed the Americans they would challenge them anywhere.

American Counterattack

At the same time that U.S. troops were heading to Vietnam, American leaders sought a peaceful end to the conflict. In the fall of 1964 President Johnson sent a message to the North Vietnamese offering to pour American dollars into a massive public works project to develop dams and hydroelectric plants along the Mekong River. The project could benefit a huge region of Southeast Asia. However, in exchange for the money the Communists would have to give up their claim to South Vietnam. After making the offer, Johnson boasted to an aide, "Old Ho can't turn that down."[8] But Ho did turn the deal down, and the attacks on U.S. positions continued.

After the Pleiku attack, Johnson resolved to get tough with the Communists. "I've gone far enough," Johnson barked to his aides. "I've had enough of this."[9] That was when Johnson ordered the commencement of Operation Rolling Thunder, a series of bombing missions to attack military targets in the North. The missions would also target the Ho Chi Minh Trail in an effort to wipe out Ho's supply line to the South. The first bombs fell on North Vietnamese targets on March 2, 1965, hitting an ammunition dump.

Under the plan for Operation Rolling Thunder, the military would not attack civilian targets. For example, the huge dikes that held the Red River back from heavily populated sections of the North were not designated as targets. If the dikes had burst, they would have released billions of gallons of water, and the resulting floods might have killed hundreds of thousands of North Vietnamese peasants. The catastrophe would certainly have thrown the Communist government into chaos and possibly destabilized the regime, but Johnson had decided early in the war to spare the civilian population. Still, the bombing was relentless, and although civilians were not targeted, it was inevitable that many people—such as those working in or around factories or facilities that were targeted—would die in the aerial attacks.

Some officials in Washington questioned whether the bombing campaign would be effective. They pointed out that there were few war-related industries in the North; the Soviets and Chinese were manufacturing and providing most of the weapons and military supplies used by North Vietnamese soldiers and Vietcong guerrillas. Undersecretary of State George Ball explained his perspective:

> I was convinced that we were not going to achieve our will by bombing the North; that in the first place, it was a fairly primitive industrial society, and that there weren't the kind of targets that were adapted for strategic bombing. And secondly, I was convinced that we would never break the will of a determined people by simply bombing; and in fact, we would probably tend to unite them more than ever.[10]

The Ho Chi Minh Trail

The Ho Chi Minh Trail was established to equip the Communist guerillas in South Vietnam with arms, ammunition, and other supplies. The trail was not a single passageway but a network of dirt roads and paths that twisted their way down from North Vietnam, through parts of Laos and Cambodia, into South Vietnam. To the North Vietnamese the trail was known as the Truong Sun Road, after the chain of mountains that it passed through.

The trail was opened in 1959 by a North Vietnamese Army engineering unit but little used until 1963, when North Vietnamese colonel Bui Tin spent five months exploring the trail. He determined that it had enormous potential as a supply route for the poorly armed and organized Vietcong. Soon dozens of trucks carrying supplies were being driven down the trail each week. They were guided by guerillas who knew every turn, river crossing, and hazard along its 2,000 miles (3,218km).

The trail was well hidden by the dense jungle. Over the years the North Vietnamese and Vietcong improved the route, widening the tiny dirt roads and paving its entire length.

A North Vietnamese peasant carries supplies down the Ho Chi Minh Trail.

Adding to the difficulties of the Americans and South Vietnamese was the fact that the Americans could not easily cut off the supply of war matériel from the North to the South. The Ho Chi Minh Trail was not a single road but a network of paths and small dirt roads that snaked through the jungle. These trails were well hidden by the heavy jungle foliage and were therefore virtually impossible to spot from the air. Each week dozens of North Vietnamese trucks guided by guerillas rolled along the trail, bringing arms, ammunition, and other supplies to the Vietcong insurgents in the South.

Avoiding Full-Scale War

The first American ground troops arrived on March 8, 1965, when thirty-five hundred marines landed at Da Nang to protect an air base located near the coastal city. By the end of the year, two hundred thousand American troops were stationed in South Vietnam.

A handful of American allies sent troops to Vietnam. Among them were South Korea, Thailand, Australia, New Zealand, and the Philippines. Leaders of these Pacific Rim countries believed they had the most to fear if China or the Soviet Union gained influence over Southeast Asia. However, South Vietnam and the United States carried the burden of supplying most of the manpower for the war. To provide troops for the military, the U.S. Congress reinstituted the draft—an action that would prove to be very unpopular with Americans. Draft resistance commenced

South Vietnamese soldiers hold a group of suspected Vietcong guerillas at gunpoint. Such actions only seemed to help strengthen the Vietcong's resolve to oppose the government forces.

as soon as the first young men were called to military service, and by the middle of 1965, 380 American men had been arrested for refusing military induction.

With the addition of the draftees, the American military soon had enough troops in Southeast Asia to wage a full-scale invasion of North Vietnam. However, in late 1965 Chinese leaders warned Johnson that if the American military sent troops across the 17th parallel, China would send its army to defend North Vietnam. This would turn the conflict into a full-scale war between two major powers. Johnson thought it best to heed the warning from the Chinese, and so he told his commanders not to invade North Vietnam. Instead, the American strategy was to bomb military targets in the North and root out Communist guerillas in the South.

This mission took American troops into rural villages, where they searched for any evidence of Vietcong involvement. Suspected guerillas were taken into custody, and any hut with hidden weapons or ammunition was burned to the ground. The strategy was at first successful, forcing the Vietcong further into the jungle, but American military leaders failed to realize that every time their soldiers burned down a hut they drove more peasants into the ranks of the enemy. In 1965 *CBS News* reporter Morley Safer reported on one such operation in the village of Cam Se:

> The day's operation burned down 150 houses, wounded three women, killed one baby, wounded one Marine and netted four prisoners. Four old men who could not answer questions put to them in English. Four old men who had no idea what an I.D. card was. Today's operation is the frustration of Vietnam in miniature. There is little doubt that American firepower can win a military victory here. But to a Vietnamese peasant whose home is a— means a lifetime of backbreaking labor—it will take more than presidential promises to convince him that we are on his side.[11]

The Americans had to carry the brunt of the fighting because it soon became clear to the U.S. military that the South Vietnamese army, known as the Army of the Republic of Vietnam (ARVN), was not effective. The Vietcong soon realized this as well. For years the Vietcong had conducted a guerilla campaign, but in 1965 the guerillas started forming into regiments and attacking the South Vietnamese in direct combat. In May 1965 Vietcong regiments overran South Vietnamese units in Songbe, some 50 miles (80km) from Saigon, and in Quang Ngai, a city along the coast. The ARVN's worst defeat was suffered at the town of Dong Xoia, where some eight hundred South Vietnamese soldiers were killed in a Vietcong raid.

Bill Ehrhart, a Pennsylvania man who served in the U.S. Marines, described what he saw as a tremendous difference between the courageous Vietcong and the soldiers of the ARVN. He said:

> One of the first things that I began to wonder about—really wonder about—is the soldiers who were our

A soldier dumps a bag of confiscated rice into an irrigation ditch. Actions like these helped alienate peasants from the South Vietnamese.

allies, the Army of the Republic. . . . They wouldn't fight! At least in our area, in heavily populated civilian areas where the enemy was literally the old farmer-by-day, fighter-by-night kind of thing. With virtually no equipment except what they could capture from the Americans and the ARVN, tremendously outnumbered, the Vietcong were there day after day picking away at us. You know, like gophers at the feet of a buffalo or something. And it occurred to me that these are the same people. The ARVN and the Vietcong are the same people, the same race, the same culture, and yet one side seems to be chicken and the other side seems to fight in the face of overwhelming disadvantages.[12]

William C. Westmoreland

General William C. Westmoreland commanded American forces in Vietnam from 1964 until 1968, when he was promoted to Army Chief of Staff—the top post in the U.S. Army. Born in 1914 in Spartanburg, South Carolina, Westmoreland had ancestors who had fought for the South in the U.S. Civil War. When Westmoreland made it clear he intended to attend the U.S. Military Academy at West Point, New York—the same school attended by the generals Grant and Sherman—a great uncle told him, "All right son—Robert E. Lee and Stonewall Jackson went there, too."

Under Westmoreland's command, American forces were never defeated in combat. Nevertheless, confidence in his leadership was shaken by the ferocity of the North Vietnamese army and Vietcong attacks waged during the Tet Offensive, which came shortly after Westmoreland boasted that the enemy was losing in a war of attrition.

Westmoreland retired from the army in 1972 and ran unsuccessfully for governor of South Carolina two years later. In 1982 *CBS News* produced a documentary alleging that Westmoreland had withheld the truth about Vietcong troop strength. Westmoreland sued the network, and the case was settled when CBS issued an apology to the general. Westmoreland died in 2005 at the age of ninety-one.

Quoted in Michael Maclear, *The Ten Thousand Day War: Vietnam, 1945–1975*. New York: St. Martin's, 1981, p. 155.

Bringing Stability to the South

For the next two years U.S. soldiers fought guerrillas in the South while American bombers continued to pound targets in the North. (Johnson did occasionally order brief halts to the air war in an effort to lure the North Vietnamese to the bargaining table, but these overtures were not successful.) American troop escalations continued as well. By early 1967 the United States had more than 360,000 troops stationed in South Vietnam.

Other changes had been taking place in South Vietnam during this time. Notably, a stable government had finally been put into place. After the 1963 overthrow of Diem's regime, a series of military commanders had taken control of South Vietnam's government. Most were corrupt leaders who lacked the support of the people; one general, Pham Xuan Chieu, admitted, "We are very weak politically and without the strong political support of the population which the [Vietcong] have."[13] But in 1967 the South

Vietnamese staged an election and selected Nguyen Van Thieu as president. A career military officer and member of the Viet Minh who had fought against the French and Japanese, Thieu had resigned from the movement when Ho sought the backing of the Soviets and Chinese. Although during his presidency Thieu's administration faced accusations of corruption, Thieu nevertheless governed with the popular support of the South Vietnamese.

Near the end of 1967 the American commander in Vietnam, General William Westmoreland, delivered a rosy prediction about the progress of the war, suggesting that the tide had turned in favor of the Americans and South Vietnamese. Visiting Washington, D.C., in November 1967, Westmoreland told journalists that the United States had contained the Vietcong guerillas, slowed the shipment of arms and supplies to the Vietcong in the South, and that the bombing campaign in the North had worn down the will of the Communists to fight. "It is significant that the enemy has not won a major battle in more than a year," Westmoreland boasted. "In general, he can fight his large forces only at the edges of his sanctuaries. His guerilla force is declining at a steady rate." [14]

Other officials echoed those remarks. During a visit to Saigon, Vice President Hubert Humphrey told reporters, "We are beginning to win this struggle. We are on the offensive. Territory is being gained. We are making steady progress." [15] Yet

events that unfolded in the next few weeks proved Humphrey, Westmoreland, and the other supporters of the war effort terribly wrong.

The Tet Offensive

Even as Westmoreland told reporters that the end of the war was in sight, his subordinates in South Vietnam were monitoring massive troop movements in the North, which suggested that the North was planning a major offensive. On January 21, 1968, the Communists struck, targeting a U.S. Marine air base at Khe Sanh, just below the 17th parallel. The attack

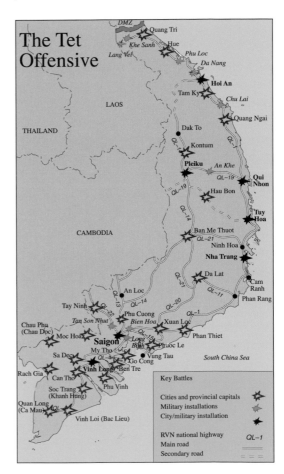

Key Battles of the Tet Offensive.

was significant because it was waged not by Vietcong guerillas but by a force of twenty thousand soldiers from the army of North Vietnam. It was the first time in the war that the North Vietnamese Army had directly confronted American troops.

At first it appeared that Khe Sanh would be a repeat of the French defeat at Dien Bien Phu. There were only six thousand marines to hold the base. However, the American soldiers withstood the attack, supported by an effective pinpoint bombing campaign that drove the North Vietnamese army away from Khe Sanh.

The siege of Khe Sanh was not an isolated attack. For months the Communists had been planning a major assault on South Vietnam that they hoped would turn the tide of the war in their favor. The prime thrust of the siege would be the major cities of the South, including Saigon, where Vietcong guerillas intended to confront defenders head-on and, they hoped, stir up passions among the South Vietnamese for liberation. North Vietnamese leaders believed that the Americans were unpopular in the South and that once southern city dwellers saw an offensive take place against the Americans, these citizens would join their fight against the Americans as well.

Khe Sanh was a diversionary strike. North Vietnamese military leaders hoped the United States would rush troops north to defend the base, thereby leaving Saigon and the other targeted cities with fewer defenders. Even though the U.S. military did not follow this plan, instead electing to break the siege of Khe Sanh using air power, the North Vietnamese army com-

manders decided to proceed with their original plan. On January 31 the North Vietnamese army and Vietcong launched a series of coordinated attacks that commenced during Tet, a Vietnamese holiday that marks the beginning of the Lunar New Year.

The Battle for Hue

Throughout the war both sides had always respected Tet with a cease-fire, but in 1968 the North Vietnamese generals decided to seize the element of surprise by attacking during the holiday. The attacks, which became known as the Tet Offensive, eventually lasted some five months. Approximately sixty cities and smaller communities in the South were targeted, but the major fighting was waged in Saigon and the city of Hue just north of Da Nang.

One of Vietnam's most historic cities, Hue was at one time the capital of the Nguyen dynasty, which had ruled Vietnam from the seventeenth to nineteenth centuries. Hue features many pagoda-style buildings, including the sprawling palace known as the Citadel, and was always regarded as the most cosmopolitan city in Vietnam, thanks in part to its many open-air cafés, gourmet restaurants, ornate palaces, and striking outdoor statuary.

When the Tet Offensive began, Hue was protected by South Vietnamese troops. The North Vietnamese army and Vietcong guerillas met little resistance at first, overrunning the city on January 31. They arrested government officials, police officers, and thousands of civilians sus-

The city of Hue lies in ruin after a twenty-six-day battle between the South Vietnamese and the Vietcong.

pected of collaborating with the Americans. Most of those arrested would receive no mercy from the Communists. As many as three thousand civilians were murdered, their bodies thrown into shallow graves. Later, when the graves were dug up, many of the victims were found to have been shot in the head while their hands were tied behind their backs.

U.S. commanders decided not to repel the attack on Hue with an air strike because they did not want to damage the many historic buildings in the city. Instead, they dispatched U.S. Army and U.S. Marine battalions to the city. As they approached the city from the south, the American troops came under heavy fire. For the next twenty-six days, the Battle of Hue was fought street by street, house by house, in some of the most fierce fighting of the Vietnam War. By the time the Communist troops were driven out of the city,

Eddie Adams and the Tet Photo

One of the most horrific images from the Tet Offensive was a photograph taken on February 1, 1968, as Vietcong guerillas swarmed into Saigon streets as part of the Tet Offensive. In the photo General Nguyen Ngoc Loan, the chief of the South Vietnamese national police, executes a Vietcong guerilla. Only minutes earlier, the guerilla had murdered a policeman and his family. The photograph captures the moment that Loan fires a pistol into the head of his grimacing prisoner.

The photograph, published on the front pages of newspapers throughout the United States and other countries, had a chilling effect on newspaper readers, who suddenly saw vivid evidence of the brutality of the Vietnam War. In 1969 American news photographer Eddie Adams won the Pulitzer Prize for this photo. The Pulitzer Prize is America's most prestigious award for journalism.

Adams later said he had seen the guerilla led out of a building by police officers. He hurried over and raised his camera, thinking the picture would simply be a routine photograph of a man taken prisoner. Suddenly, Loan approached the prisoner. "I was about five feet away from him and I see him reach for his pistol," Adams said. "I thought he was going to threaten the prisoner. So as quick as he brought his pistol up, I took a picture. But it turned out he shot him."

Quoted in Al Santoli, *To Bear Any Burden: The Vietnam War and Its Aftermath in the Words of Americans and Southeast Asians.* Bloomington: Indiana University Press, 1999.

---

some 8,000 North Vietnamese and Vietcong fighters had been killed. Besides the 3,000 civilians who had been massacred by the Communists, several thousand more were killed in the crossfire. In addition 384 South Vietnamese and 216 American troops lost their lives.

"Throughout all of this, you constantly had this fear," said U.S. Marine Captain Myron Harrington, who fought in the Battle of Hue. "You had this utter devastation all around you. You had this horrible smell. I mean you just cannot describe the smell of death especially when you're looking at it a couple of weeks along."[16]

The historic city of Hue was virtually leveled during the battle. Of the more than seventeen thousand homes in Hue, more than half were destroyed, while another three thousand sustained serious damage. In addition shelling damaged many of the city's pagodas and palaces, particularly the Citadel, which the North Vietnamese army had used as a base. When journalist Robert Shaplen toured the city after the fighting, he wrote, "Nothing I saw during the Korean War, or in the Vietnam War so far, has been as terrible, in terms of destruction and despair, as what I saw in Hue."[17]

Resolve of the Communists

Strategically, the Tet Offensive was a disaster for the North Vietnamese army. Civilians in South Vietnam did not rally behind the Communist cause as North Vietnamese leaders had expected. Furthermore, the North Vietnamese army and Vietcong sustained heavy casualties and gained no new territory. Their attacks in Saigon were particularly fruitless. At one point Vietcong guerillas captured a radio station in Saigon with the intention of broadcasting a taped message from Ho calling for the liberation of the city. Moments after the guerillas captured the station, however, the power to the building was cut off, thwarting their plans. At the end of the siege, eight guerillas inside the building detonated a bomb, destroying the radio station and taking their own lives.

An equally disastrous siege was laid against the U.S. embassy in Saigon. A group of Vietcong guerillas attacked the embassy, blowing a hole in the wall of the compound and entering the embassy grounds. They drove the marine guards inside, but because their commanders had been killed in the firefight, the remaining guerillas did not know how to proceed. Instead of pressing the attack, they milled around on the grounds. Minutes later American reinforcements arrived and wiped them out.

The embassy siege and other attacks made during the Tet Offensive may not have represented military victories for the North Vietnamese, but they proved to Americans that after some three years of warfare, the resolve of the Communists had not diminished. To Johnson it became abundantly clear that the war was not winnable. On the other hand Johnson felt that he could not pull out and abandon South Vietnam to its fate. On March 31, 1968, two months after the start of the Tet Offensive, Johnson shocked Americans by announcing he would not seek re-election.

Chapter Three

Struggle in the United States

et may have been a military defeat for North Vietnam, but the offensive helped spark an intense antiwar movement in the United States. On their television sets Americans saw scenes of the fierce street-by-street fighting in Saigon and Hue. They wondered how Vietnam had become the center of the campaign against global communism and why the fight there was worth such a steep toll in human life. Prior to the Tet Offensive, a Gallup Organization poll indicated that 24 percent of Americans opposed the war. In March 1968, after some two months of fighting, Gallup reported that opposition to the war had grown to 42 percent.

One of the people who changed his perspective about the war was Walter Cronkite, the enormously popular anchor of the evening newscasts on the CBS television network. A month after the Tet Offensive began, Cronkite toured the war zone and returned with a much dimmer outlook on the prospects for victory than he had originally had. On the evening of February 27, 1968, Cronkite concluded his newscast with a call for the U.S. government to find a way to withdraw from Vietnam. "To say that we are mired in stalemate seems the only realistic, yet unsatisfactory, conclusion," Cronkite said. "It is increasingly clear to this reporter that the only rational way out then will be to negotiate, not as victors, but as an honorable people who lived up to their pledge to defend democracy, and did the best they could." [18] Watching the newscast in the White House, President Johnson turned to an aide and said, "If I've lost Cronkite, I've lost Middle America." [19]

In the coming months political leaders in Washington would fall under increasing pressure from the American people to find a way out of Vietnam. In Chicago that summer, rioting erupted outside the Democratic National Convention as antiwar activists called for American withdrawal. Elsewhere, students and others demonstrated against the war, often on college campuses or in front of military installations; some young men burned their draft cards and fled to Canada to avoid the draft. The war in Vietnam was still raging, but the battle for the hearts and minds of the American people had already been lost.

Walter Cronkite reports from Vietnam. After the Tet Offensive, Cronkite, along with many other Americans, began to see the Vietnam War as unwinnable.

Thousands of students march down Pennslyvania Avenue to protest the Vietnam War.

END THE
WAR

IN VIETNAM
NOW

Free Speech and Teach-ins

Protests against the war started almost immediately after the U.S. Congress passed the Gulf of Tonkin Resolution. By early 1965 antiwar activists were organizing peace demonstrations. Many of the demonstrations involved college students and other young people, who by then had discovered they held enormous power to protest unfair conditions, influence policy, and sway emotions. After the bombing campaign against North Vietnam began, student leaders on a number of campuses staged Vietnam "teach-ins." These events, in which issues of the war were debated, were often supported by a large number of faculty members. The teach-ins soon were followed by a much larger show of protest—on April 17, 1965, a new organization that called itself Students for a Democratic Society (SDS) organized a protest in Washington, D.C. Some twenty-five thousand students picketed the White House, then congregated in front of the Washington Monument for a rally.

April 17 was picked as the day for the rally because it was the first day the U.S. Selective Service Commission (later called the Selective Service System) issued draft notices to young American men who had reached the draft age of nineteen. On that day some 13,700 men received notices ordering them to report for duty. The following month another 15,100 men were drafted. More than 2 million draftees would follow them to Vietnam in the years ahead. Protests against the draft were staged. Some men gathered around bonfires and publicly burned their draft cards. Many of the protesters who refused induction into the military ended up arrested and jailed. Thousands of draft-age men fled to Canada, where they planned to wait out the war. Thousands more applied for conscientious objector status, hoping to take advantage of a section in the law that exempted from combat soldiers whose religious convictions prevented them from going to war. Conscientious objectors still had to serve, but they were given jobs in the United States—usually as aides in Veterans Administration (VA) hospitals.

At first the American public supported the Vietnam War. Johnson and other U.S. leaders had made the case that Vietnam could not be allowed to fall to communism. Still, not all national leaders supported this position. In 1967 Reverend Martin Luther King Jr., the nation's most important civil rights leader at the time, announced his opposition to the war. At the time many young men avoided the draft by maintaining their status as full-time college students—an option mostly unavailable to poor, inner-city blacks. King pointed out that the percentage of blacks drafted into the military was much higher than the total percentage of African Americans in the United States. In a speech delivered at a church in New York in 1967, King mentioned numerous reasons why the war must stop:

Somehow this madness must cease. We must stop now. I speak as a child of God and brother to the suffering poor of Vietnam. I speak for those whose land is being laid waste, whose homes are being destroyed, whose culture is being subverted. I speak for the poor of America who are paying the double price of smashed hopes at home and dealt death and corruption in Vietnam. I speak as a citizen of the world, for the world as it stands aghast at the path we have taken. I speak as an American to the leaders of my own nation. The great initiative in this war is ours; the initiative to stop it must be ours. [20]

In 1971 Congress revoked student deferments, meaning that anybody who was required to sign up for the draft could no longer stay out of the military simply by registering for college classes. College deferments had become an option that more Americans had chosen as public opinion turned against the war.

Rioting in Chicago

Following the Tet Offensive, Washington still had its hawks (a nickname for those who prefer using military force to achieve foreign policy goals), but some politicians had begun speaking out against America's involvement, voicing the country's growing frustration and anger about the war. After Johnson's decision to withdraw from the 1968 presidential contest, some candidates seeking the White House

Antiwar protestors burn their draft cards on the steps of the Pentagon during the Vietnam War.

"We Cannot Go Back"

In the April 1965 demonstration in Washington, D.C., that the Students for a Democratic Society organized, the group's leader, Paul Potter, addressed the crowd, saying:

I believe that the administration is serious about expanding the war in Asia. The question is whether the people here are as serious about ending it. I wonder what it means for each of us to say we want to end the war in Vietnam—whether, if we accept the full meaning of that statement and the gravity of the situation, we can simply leave the march and go back to the routines of a society that acts as if it were not in the midst of a grave crisis. Maybe we, like the president, are insulated from the consequences of our own decision to end the war. Maybe we have yet really to listen to the screams of a burning child and decide that we cannot go back to whatever it is we did before today until that war has ended.

Paul Potter, "Naming the System," Radical Education Project. www.radicaleducation.org/sds_ documents/paul_potter.html.

openly questioned the war and vowed that if they won the election American troops would be brought home.

The Democratic Party's leading contender for the presidency was Johnson's vice president, Hubert Humphrey, who publicly supported the war. The most vocal critic of the war was U.S. senator Eugene McCarthy, a Democrat from Minnesota. He was initially regarded as a fringe candidate without the support of his party, although he shocked political insiders by nearly beating Johnson in the New Hampshire primary, an event that helped convince Johnson not to run for president in 1968. McCarthy had been helped by thousands of student organizers who flocked to New Hampshire to work in his campaign. Four days after the New Hampshire

primary, another Democrat entered the race—Senator Robert F. Kennedy of New York. Kennedy, the younger brother of assassinated president John F. Kennedy, came out against the war and pledged to find a peaceful solution. But after winning the California primary in June 1968, Robert Kennedy was assassinated. He was the second major opponent of the war to lose his life in 1968 (King had been assassinated two months earlier).

That summer antiwar activists used the Democratic National Convention to air their concerns before an international audience. The thousands of demonstrators were met by the Chicago police, who were under orders from Mayor Richard Daley to smash the protests. On the night of August 25 rioting erupted in Grant

Park, the headquarters for the peace movement. Television cameras caught police wading into the crowd, clubbing demonstrators and tossing tear gas canisters. Police even assaulted some journalists. Abbie Hoffman, a radical leader of the antiwar movement, believed that the strong-arm tactics of the Chicago police helped convince even more Americans that U.S. involvement in the Vietnam War was a mistake. He said:

> At home, America sat down for the evening meal and turned on the TV, expecting the background sounds of political Muzak that had become the hallmark of a decided convention. Instead, they were presented with the shock of helmeted police gassing and clubbing young people to the ground. The country was instantaneously plugged and plunged into civil war. Parents fought with their kids, some of whom left home, grabbed a plane, and joined us in Chicago.[21]

The drama of Grant Park did not end a few nights later when Humphrey received the Democratic Party's nomination as its candidate for president. (Humphrey would lose the 1968 presidential election to Republican Richard Nixon.) Hoffman and seven other leaders were charged with inciting the riots. When one of the cases was severed from the rest, the remaining defendants became known as the "Chicago Seven." Their trial, which often took on a circus atmosphere as the defendants resorted to bizarre tactics and courtroom out-

bursts, would serve as another rallying point for antiwar activists.

Massacre at My Lai

As the demonstrators clashed with Chicago police, the fighting in Vietnam continued. Amid news of the bombings and jungle warfare, Americans caught another unsettling glimpse of the war when news outlets began reporting that American troops had massacred several hundred unarmed civilians in the village of My Lai.

The incident at My Lai unfolded on March 16, 1968, when some thirty members of Charlie Company from the army's Twentieth Infantry Division entered the village of My Lai in Quang Ngai province, near the northern coast of South Vietnam. My Lai was believed to be such a hotbed of Communist activity that the soldiers called it "Pinkville," a reference to the color red, which is associated with communism. Under the leadership of Lieutenant William Calley, the company was under orders to root out Vietcong guerillas. Convinced that the village was teeming with guerillas, Calley ordered a massacre. Everyone in the village—from young children to old men and women—was slaughtered. Most members of Charlie Company participated in the massacre, although a few, horrified by Calley's orders, refused to kill the unarmed civilians.

The murders were stopped when a helicopter pilot, Hugh Thompson Jr., arrived on the scene and threatened to open fire on the American soldiers if they did not stop killing the My Lai civilians. Thompson also called in other helicopters to help airlift the survivors to safety.

It took more than a year for the My Lai story to come out. At first army officials denied that U.S. soldiers had massacred civilians. Instead, the officials claimed that Charlie Company had killed 128 Vietcong guerillas and that 22 civilians had died in this battle. Within months of the slaughter, though, members of Charlie Company confided to other soldiers what had happened at My Lai. One man who heard the stories was Ronald Ridenhour, who knew many members of Charlie Company. After much soul-searching, Ridenhour wrote a fifteen-hundred-word letter out-

Roaring flames consume a house during the My Lai massacre. The deaths of hundreds of unarmed peasants in the village sparked international outrage.

lining what he heard and mailed it to the president and other high-ranking government officials, including many prominent members of Congress. The letter stated, in part:

Exactly what did in fact occur in the village of Pinkville in March 1968 I do not know for certain, but I am convinced that it was something very black indeed. I remain irrevocably persuaded that if you and I do truly believe in the principles of justice and the equality of every man, however humble, before the law, that form the very backbone that this country is founded on, then we must press forward a widespread and public investigation of this matter with all our combined efforts. [22]

One recipient of the letter was U.S. representative Morris Udall, a member of Congress from Arizona. An opponent of the war, Udall circulated Ridenhour's letter among the members of the House Armed Services Committee, which oversees the military. Soon members of Congress were demanding answers from high-ranking officials in the Defense Department. In the summer of 1969 Calley and twenty-five other members of Charlie Company were charged with the murders of civilians at My Lai.

Word Gets Out

The horrifying story of My Lai had not yet been leaked to the public, but that would change in the fall of 1969, when investigative journalist Seymour Hersh heard sto-

ries about the massacre. Hersh followed the story to Fort Benning, Georgia, where Calley was being held in the stockade pending trial. Calley gave an extensive interview to Hersh, describing the massacre and contending that members of Charlie Company had simply been following orders when they wiped out the village.

In November 1969 Hersh's story about the My Lai massacre was published in newspapers throughout the country. *Time* and *Newsweek* both obtained photographs of the dead at My Lai and used them on their covers. The images had been taken by a military photographer, but until that point their release had been suppressed by army officials.

Calley and the other soldiers went on trial in 1971. After a lengthy trial, a military court-martial convicted Calley but acquitted the other members of Charlie Company. Calley was sentenced to life in prison, but three days after the verdict was announced, President Nixon freed the lieutenant pending his appeal. Nixon reacted to an overwhelming measure of support for Calley from the American public, who believed the lieutenant had been made a scapegoat for the murders at My Lai. Calley spent the next three and a half years under house arrest at Fort Benning. When Calley's appeals ran out, Nixon granted him an immediate parole. Calley left the army and returned home to Georgia.

Critics of the war contended that My Lai was an incident waiting to happen. They suggested that since 1965, American servicemen had been exposed to the most horrific forms of killing. Also, as the My

The Twenty-sixth Amendment

The Twenty-sixth Amendment to the U.S. Constitution provides Americans who are eighteen years or older with the right to vote. Prior to the adoption of this amendment in 1971, the minimum voting age in the United States was twenty-one.

The Vietnam War was responsible for the extension of voting rights to Americans as young as eighteen. Before 1971 eighteen-year-old American men had to register for the draft but could not vote. Many contended that this was not fair. Their slogan was "Old Enough to Fight, Old Enough to Vote."

Legislators agreed with the idea, and on March 23, 1971, those in both houses of Congress passed a joint resolution lowering the voting age. The required three-quarters of the state legislatures approved the amendment on July 1, making it law. It was the fastest adoption of a constitutional amendment in American history. A year later 11 million voters under the age of twenty-one participated in their first presidential election.

Lai case unfolded, it became clear that Calley had been poorly trained and was unprepared for a leadership role in combat. Before joining the army, Calley had dropped out of college due to poor grades. He had held a number of odd jobs, including bellhop and dishwasher, before enlisting in the army in 1966. Within months he had been admitted to Officer Candidate School, then commissioned as a lieutenant. Retired colonel George Walton of the U.S. Army remarked, "When an army is required to fight a war without the support of society it is forced to commission its Calleys."[23]

A Tragic Day in Ohio

Once the public saw the photographs of the dead at My Lai and learned the grim details of the killings in late 1969, support for the war eroded steadily. By August 1971, 61 percent of respondents to a Gallup poll called for an immediate withdrawal of troops from Vietnam. This marked the first time a majority of Americans opposed the war.

Protests against the war continued. In August 1969, 500,000 young people gathered near the remote New York State town of Bethel to attend the Woodstock Music and Art Festival. The three-day rock concert turned into a giant antiwar rally, as performer after performer punctuated his or her music with political messages. Later that year, some 250,000 young Americans marched on Washington, demanding an end to the war.

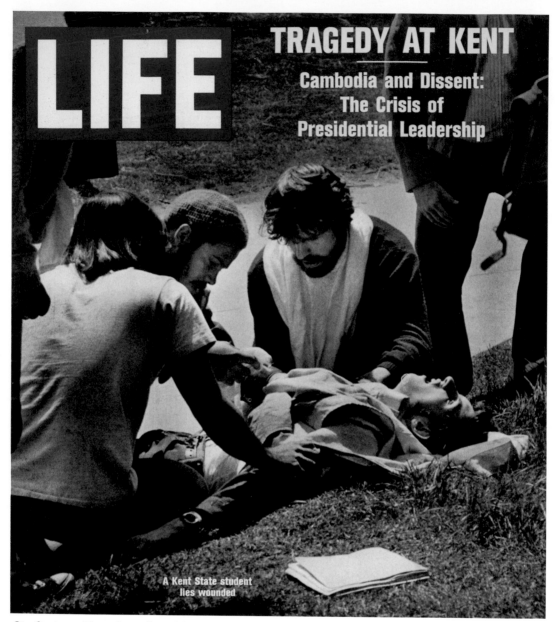

LIFE

TRAGEDY AT KENT

Cambodia and Dissent:
The Crisis of
Presidential Leadership

A Kent State student
lies wounded

Students at Kent State kneel beside John Cleary, who was one of the students struck by a National Guardsman's bullets in the event that came to be known as the Kent State Massacre.

But on May 4, 1970, violence occurred at an antiwar protest at Kent State University in Ohio. The eighty-four hundred students that had gathered for the rally there were met by fidgety National Guardsmen. When some students started pelting the soldiers with stones, the guardsmen at first retreated, but then they turned and fired on the protestors. Four students were killed and nine were wounded. Americans were shocked when they saw photographs of the incident—one famous picture depicted a teenage girl wailing over the body of a dead student—and the shootings sparked protests at other campuses.

Serious Complications

While antiwar protests continued in the United States, other Americans were returning home from Vietnam as veterans of the war. Unfortunately, these Vietnam veterans discovered that the American public did not wish to regard them as heroes. With the war losing support, veterans were easy targets for criticism. Antiwar protestors denounced the soldiers as "baby killers," and many of the veterans later admitted that this treatment made their return to civilian life very difficult.

Many of those who returned from Vietnam also suffered psychological and phys-

Long after the war ended, this Vietnam vet shows the lasting agony and pain that continued to plague the veterans of the war. Unlike the veterans of most previous American wars, Vietnam veterans were never regarded by the public as heroes.

ical problems related to their service. One of the more common complications was post-traumatic stress disorder, a psychological condition triggered by stressful episodes in the person's life. The disorder can manifest itself through nightmares, insomnia, flashbacks, memory loss, depression, and other mental illnesses. Some veterans found themselves acting irrationally because a stressful memory from their Vietnam service was suddenly jarred loose in their minds. Following the war, studies showed that as many as 30 percent of Vietnam veterans suffered post-traumatic stress disorder at least once.

Aside from post-traumatic stress, other problems afflicted veterans. Some three hundred thousand Americans were disabled to some degree by the wounds they received in the war. Additionally, some veterans later contracted cancer and other illnesses because they had been exposed to Agent Orange during their tours in Vietnam. Agent Orange is a chemical used to defoliate jungles. It was sprayed in abundance to burn the heavy foliage away from villages, military bases, and other installations to deny hiding places to Vietcong guerillas.

Another problem that many Vietnam veterans later had to deal with was hepatitis C, a disease of the blood. Hepatitis C has long been widespread in Southeast Asia; medical researchers have concluded that soldiers who received blood transfusions during the war may have been infected with hepatitis C because of the unsanitary conditions on the battlefields. In many cases hepatitis C takes some thirty years before the disease emerges. The disease eventually can lead to liver failure and death.

Plight of the POWs

Although many veterans returned home and had to cope with new issues, a few servicemen found themselves virtually forgotten. They were prisoners of war (POWs) held by the North Vietnamese in camps or jails that were cramped, dark, and unsanitary. Most of the prisoners of war were pilots who had been shot down while on bombing missions over the North. These prisoners were fed the minimum amount of food to keep them alive and were subjected to constant beatings and other tortures.

In 1969 reports started leaking out about North Vietnam's brutal treatment of prisoners—how they were led through the streets of Hanoi and paraded in front of Vietnamese people who called them killers and pelted them with rocks. Some unfortunate pilots were held for months or even years in "tiger cages"—bamboo cages in the jungle, some not even large enough to stand in. Most of the other prisoners were held in more than a dozen filthy prisons in the North, where they shared their cells with rats and had to endure constant interrogations and beatings by guards. Most were forced to sign propaganda statements or appear in crude films claiming their bombing missions had been criminal.

Pilots frequently were injured when they were shot down, suffering broken bones and other wounds. When these soldiers were captured, the North Vietnamese provided medical care, but it was

Inhumane Conditions

In 1949 during the First Indochina War, North Vietnam had signed the Geneva Conventions, a treaty that specified that all prisoners of war were to be treated humanely. During the Second Indochina War, or the Vietnam War, the North Vietnamese at first insisted that American prisoners were being held under humane conditions, as had been promised. They showcased POWs at a prison known as the Plantation, which once had been a mansion occupied by the mayor of Hanoi. The facility had clean cells and gardens tilled by the inmates. Whenever foreign human rights dignitaries demanded to see the POW conditions in North Vietnam, they were given tours of the Plantation.

But when news of the true conditions in the North Vietnamese prisons leaked out, the Communists assumed a new stance: They insisted that since America had never formally declared war on North Vietnam, the Americans were not prisoners of war but war criminals. The rationale did not matter, though; the North Vietnamese still were assailed by intense international pressure to improve conditions for the POWs. Eventually, the prisoners' food and medical care improved and the torture ceased.

rudimentary at best. North Vietnamese doctors would set broken ankles, for example, but painkillers were unheard of. Infections were common and so were diseases contracted in the jungle or in prison, among them malaria and dysentery. Food usually consisted of meager rations of rice, noodles, and watery soup.

Interrogation was always a part of the routine in the North Vietnamese prisons. Interrogators wanted to know about American war plans and military organization. When the pilots refused to talk, they were tortured. Many were beaten with fists or rifle butts or whipped with rubber strips. To induce pain, their arms or legs were stretched with rope. Navy

pilot John McCain, who would later become a senator from Arizona, was captured in 1967 when his plane was shot down over Hanoi. He broke a leg and two arms in the crash and spent six years as a POW. McCain described his experience in an interrogation room:

At two-to-three-hour intervals, the guards returned to administer beatings. The intensity of the punishment varied from visit to visit depending on the energy and enthusiasm of the guards. Still, I felt they were being careful not to kill or permanently injure me. One guard would hold me while the others pounded away. Most blows were directed at my shoulders, chest and stomach. Occasionally, when I had fallen to the floor, they kicked me in the head. They cracked several of my ribs and broke a couple of teeth. My bad right leg was swollen and hurt most of any of my injuries. Weakened by beatings and dysentery, and with my right leg again nearly useless, I found it almost impossible to stand. [24]

Unlike many of the soldiers who returned from Vietnam, McCain and 590 other POWs released by the North Vietnamese in early 1973 came home to a warm embrace by Americans. The plight of these prisoners had become well known in the United States, and Americans were anxious to show their appreciation to the veterans who had endured the worst of the war. McCain recalled:

> During our captivity, the Vietnamese had inundated us with information about how unpopular the war and the men who fought it had become with the American public. We were stunned and relieved to discover that most Americans were as happy to see us as we were to see them. A lot of us were overcome by our reception, and the affection we were shown helped us to begin putting the war behind us. [25]

Chapter Four

"Peace Is at Hand"

By the spring of 1968, President Johnson's strategy of bombing Hanoi and then ordering brief respites from the air strikes finally seemed to have worked, since Communist leaders agreed, albeit reluctantly, to begin peace talks. On May 10 diplomats from North Vietnam and the United States met in Paris to begin negotiations for the cease-fire. It appeared as though this long and bloody war was grinding to a halt at last.

But the euphoria felt by the diplomats when they sat down across the bargaining table soon gave way to rancor, stalling, and squabbling. It became painfully clear that neither side was willing to give ground.

In November 1968 a new U.S. president, Richard M. Nixon, was elected. During the presidential campaign, Nixon had insisted that he had a secret plan to end the war. In early 1969 Nixon made his plan clear: He ordered stepped-up bombing of the North in an effort to force the Communists to give concessions at the Paris peace talks. In the meantime Nixon also expanded the war into Laos and Cambodia, bombing and raiding camps and villages the North Vietnamese were using to stage raids into South Vietnam.

After the Tet Offensive, Americans had no more patience for the bloody street fighting that had dominated the war for the first half of 1968. Another element of Nixon's solution was to start phasing out American troops, thereby turning over the ground war to the South Vietnamese. For years, the South Vietnamese soldiers had failed to prove themselves in combat, but once the Americans started leaving, the ARVN stepped up to the task and proved to be a resilient fighting force. Even so, it would take until early 1973 before Nixon finally withdrew all American troops from Vietnam.

The Madman Theory

In 1968 Americans endured a bitter campaign for the presidency. Vice President

Hubert Humphrey won the Democratic nomination at the tumultuous party convention in Chicago that summer, but as a member of the Johnson administration he was forced to support the war. Only within the final few weeks of the campaign did Johnson release the reins on Humphrey and permit him to speak for himself. Making a peace initiative, Humphrey immediately called for a halt to all bombing in the North.

The Republican nominee was Nixon, a former vice president and fierce anticommunist. As peace talks got underway in Paris, Nixon sent an emissary to South Vietnamese president Nguyen Van Thieu, urging Thieu not to participate in the negotiations. The emissary assured Thieu that the South would get a better deal from Nixon than from either Johnson or Humphrey. Thieu agreed, and South Vietnam stayed out of the talks. Without South

Nixon greets soldiers in Vietnam. He had hoped to use the threat of nuclear war to bring the North Vietnamese back to the negotiating table.

Vietnam's participation, any hope for a quick resolution in Paris was doomed.

As the U.S. presidential campaigning continued into the fall, Nixon enjoyed a tremendous lead in the polls, but that advantage soon evaporated as Humphrey promoted his plan to end the war. However, despite Humphrey's commitment to end the war, the Democrat faced a hostile electorate weary of the Johnson administration's management of the conflict. The election ended in a narrow victory for Nixon. Experts believe many antiwar voters simply stayed home on election day. These voters felt that neither Humphrey nor Nixon would agree to an immediate cessation of hostilities.

Contrary to what the newly elected president had announced during his campaign, Nixon had no secret plan to end the war. As vice president during the final year of the Korean War, Nixon had watched as President Eisenhower threatened to use nuclear weapons on the North Koreans unless they agreed to a cease-fire. The strategy had worked. Now as president, Nixon intended to use virtually the same strategy on the North Vietnamese—he would threaten the use of nuclear weapons and ratchet up the bombing campaign to force the Communists to submit to his terms. Nixon explained the strategy to Bob Haldeman, his chief of staff:

I call it the Madman Theory, Bob. I want the North Vietnamese to believe that I've reached the point where I might do anything to stop the war. We'll just slip the word to them that,

"for God's sake, you know Nixon is obsessed about Communists. We can't restrain him when he's angry— and he has his hand on the nuclear button"—and Ho Chi Minh himself will be in Paris in two days begging for peace.[26]

Nixon stepped up the bombing campaign, but the North Vietnamese remained resolute. At the same time Nixon also kept his promise to reduce the number of American soldiers in South Vietnam, which now stood at more than five hundred thousand. By the end of 1969 the United States dropped the strength of its force by sixty thousand men. Further reductions would be ordered in the coming years.

Opportunity for Peace

Even as the U.S. ground troops withdrew, the bombing in the North continued. Nixon tested his madman theory by sending a message to officials in the North threatening an even more massive bombing campaign unless they agreed to withdraw their claims on the South. On September 2, 1969, while Communist leaders considered the ramifications of Nixon's threat, Ho Chi Minh died at the age of seventy-nine. Congress called on Nixon to engage in serious peace talks with the North, suggesting that Ho's death offered a great opportunity for peace because a new generation of North Vietnamese leaders might be more willing to give ground.

That was not likely to happen, however. In North Vietnam the entire nation

Drugs in Vietnam

A merican soldiers stationed in South Vietnam found they had little trouble obtaining illegal drugs. Marijuana was readily available from street dealers in Saigon and other cities. So were other drugs, including heroin, opium, methamphetamines (also known as speed), and lysergic acid diethylamide (also known as LSD or acid).

In 1971 a study authorized by Congress found that drugs had become a major problem in the military, undermining the ability of many units to fight. The study estimated that roughly thirty thousand American soldiers serving in Vietnam were addicted to heroin.

Army private George Cantero recalled the ease with which he could obtain drugs in an article on Vietnam Online. "For a box of Tide [laundry detergent], you could get a carton of pre-packed, pre-rolled marijuana cigarettes soaked in opium," he wrote. "For $10 you could get a vial of pure heroin about the size of . . . a cigarette butt. And, you could get liquid opium, speed, acid, anything you wanted."

Quoted in *The American Experience,* PBS, "Vietnam Online." www.pbs.org/wgbh/amex/vietnam/series/pt_07.html.

---

mourned the death of the beloved Uncle Ho, the only leader its people had known since 1945. For months, Ho had been ailing and aware he did not have long to live. On the day of his death, the Communist government released a statement that Ho had written just a few months before, urging the North Vietnamese people to endure the air strikes. The statement read, in part:

> Our compatriots in the North and the South shall be reunited under the same roof. We, a small nation, will have earned the unique honor of defeating, through a heroic struggle, two big imperialisms—the French and the American—and making a worthy contribution to the national liberation movement. . . . To the whole people, the whole [Communist] party, the whole army, to my nephews and nieces, the youth and children, I leave my boundless love."[27]

The North Vietnamese would not capitulate, so Nixon ordered the bombing to resume. In 1969 Nixon also directed the air force to bomb North Vietnamese army strongholds in neighboring Cambodia, thus widening the war.

The War Spreads into Laos and Cambodia

For years Cambodia and its neighbor to the north, Laos, had been indirectly involved in the Vietnam War, because the Ho Chi Minh Trail crossed their territories. Cambodia's leader, Prince Norodom Sihanouck, had negotiated with China, France, Indonesia, and other countries with influence in Asia to maintain neutrality during the conflict, but by 1969 the North Vietnamese army and Vietcong had established bases along Cambodia's 500-mile border (805km) with South Vietnam, using them to launch attacks on the South. However, in an effort to keep the war confined to Vietnam, the United States had not attacked enemy positions in Cambodia.

Nixon threw aside this strategy. He was convinced that by knocking out these bases in Cambodia he could seriously hamper the ability of the Vietcong and North Vietnamese Army to attack the South. In 1969 Nixon secretly ordered bombing raids on targets in Cambodia, and on April 30, 1970, he sent American troops into Cambodia.

On the surface, the intense military campaign was effective, forcing the North Vietnamese to shut down their bases along the border. But instead of driving the Communists back to the North, the military campaign drove them further into Cambodia, where they could assist a group of insurgents who were trying to topple Sihanouck's government. Eventu-

U.S. troops witness a bombing in Cambodia. Nixon actually expanded the war in Vietnam by allowing ground forces and air raids into the bordering country.

ally, a group known as the Khmer Rouge would win a guerilla war in Cambodia and plunge the country into one of the most horrific periods of genocide in world history.

Meanwhile, Laos faced its own insurgency. In fact, the United States had been carrying on a secret war in Laos since the early 1960s. The country was governed by a shaky coalition that included members of the Pathet Lao, the Communist organization in Laos. In the countryside Pathet Lao guerillas armed by the North Vietnamese battled Hmong tribesmen, who were armed by the U.S. Central Intelligence Agency (CIA). The CIA ferried arms and supplies to the Hmong and conducted air reconnaissance missions with planes from a phony airline, Air America, which it had established in Asia. The Hmong tribesmen were courageous warriors and managed to fight the Pathet Lao to a stalemate until the early 1970s.

Unfortunately, the Laotian military, the Royal Lao Army, was largely ineffective. Historians David Wise and Thomas B. Ross explained, "In battle, to the dismay of their American advisers, they were accustomed to aiming high in the expectation that the enemy would respond in kind."[28] As a result, the Communists had free rein to establish camps along South Vietnam's border with Laos. In early 1971 South Vietnamese and American troops started conducting raids into Laos, driving the Communists into the interior. Communist troops based in Laos would cease posing a threat to South Vietnam, but the Pathet Lao soon became a dominant force in Laos.

Vietnamization

In the United States antiwar activists denounced Nixon for spreading the war into Laos and Cambodia while publicly proclaiming for months that he was seeking an end to the conflict. Congress also demanded an end to the bombing of Cambodia. In response Nixon insisted that he was winding down the war. He did follow through on his promise to bring troops home—by the end of 1970 American troop strength in the South would be cut to some 280,000 soldiers, and by early 1972 there were just 70,000 American soldiers in South Vietnam.

As U.S. troop strength was reduced, the South Vietnamese army was called on to carry more of the fight on its own. Nixon called this transfer of responsibility to the South Vietnamese "Vietnamization." For years American commanders had questioned the will of the South Vietnamese soldiers to fight. By the late 1960s the strength of the South Vietnamese army stood at 1 million members—but some two thousand soldiers deserted each week. Once the Americans started withdrawing ground troops, though, the South Vietnamese soldiers responded with courage and fortitude.

On March 30, 1972, the Communists initiated the largest offensive since Tet in 1968. Approximately 120,000 North Vietnamese and Vietcong troops attacked three strategic regions of the South: the Mekong Delta in the far southern portion of the country; the Central Highlands; and Quang Tri, South Vietnam's northernmost province.

A group of students stands outside the ruins of their school in Quang Tri, a city heavily bombed by U.S. forces in 1972.

The most intense fighting was in Quang Tri. Refugees streamed out of the province and its capital, the city of Quang Tri. The government of South Vietnam rushed troops north. They were aided by U.S. air power, but no American ground troops participated in the battle.

At first the Communists took the city and its surrounding province. The fight-ing raged for more than five months, but on September 15 the South Vietnamese retook the capital. American air power had been instrumental in rooting out the enemy. One reporter who toured Quang Tri after it was retaken by the South said the city had been virtually destroyed in the bombing campaign. Quang Tri, he wrote, "is no longer a city but a lake of

Bob Hope in Vietnam

Each year American comedian Bob Hope staged a variety show that toured American military outposts. Hope's shows had entertained troops during World War II and the Korean War, but the nine Christmas-season shows he produced for soldiers in South Vietnam from 1964 to 1972 made Hope into an American icon, mostly because the shows were filmed and rebroadcast on American television. The show produced from Hope's 1970 tour was extremely popular, and 64 percent of all households in the United States watched it.

The shows always opened with Hope strutting onto the stage, where he would crack jokes about American politicians, military leaders, and others in the news. He was followed by a full-scale extravaganza of singers, dancers, and other performers, including such stars of the time as Ann-Margret, Raquel Welch, Phyllis Diller, Lola Falana, and Jim Nabors. Among the other celebrities who made the tours were baseball star Johnny Bench and astronaut Neil Armstrong.

Chicago newspaper columnist Irv Kupcinet once described Hope as "Uncle Sam, Santa Claus and a letter from home all wrapped up in one neat package of hilarity." Many years after the Vietnam War, in 1990 at the age of eighty-seven, Hope organized a tour of military installations in Saudi Arabia as the United States prepared to oust the Iraqis from Kuwait in Operation Desert Storm. Hope died in 2003, two months after he reached the age of one hundred.

Quoted in Timothy M. Gray and Richard Natale, "Hope and Joy," *Variety,* August 4, 2003, p. 45.

Bob Hope shakes hands with soldiers in Vietnam during his 1964 Christmas show. Hope became a household name in America for his support of American troops during many wars.

masonry. Even the thick citadel walls were so thoroughly smashed one could no longer see where they had stood."[29] More than five thousand South Vietnamese soldiers lost their lives, although not a single American was killed.

The Phoenix Program

While the United States continued its air support for the ARVN as well as an intense bombing campaign in the North, some American advisers also instructed the South Vietnamese in an effective but darkly sinister series of arrests of suspected Communists. It became known as the Phoenix Program.

The program was initially put into use in 1968 following the Tet Offensive. Under direction from the CIA, South Vietnamese agents—most of them drafted from rural villages—started scouring the countryside, rounding up suspected Vietcong guerillas and their civilian sympathizers. At first the program offered amnesty to the Vietcong: Those who turned themselves in and turned over their weapons would be free from retribution. More than seventeen thousand guerillas surrendered under those terms.

Soon, though, the South Vietnamese agents became much more aggressive in tracking down guerillas. They resorted to extremist tactics such as torture and assassination to find Vietcong guerillas and force them into the open. Eventually, more than three hundred thousand suspected guerillas were rounded up and thrown into jails or makeshift prison camps. Many were murdered while in custody. Many of the prisoners who were arrested were falsely accused of collaborating with the Communists. "When you grab that many bodies, you grab a lot of the wrong bodies," insisted Barton Osborne, a U.S. Army intelligence officer. "By late 1968, the Phoenix Program was not serving any legitimate function that I know of, but rather had gone so wrong that it was the vehicle by which we were getting into a bad genocide program."[30]

William Colby, the CIA station chief in Saigon, later said that he believed the Phoenix Program was successful in helping reduce the effectiveness of the Vietcong in the South. But Colby also said he had advised organizers of the program that torture was not an effective means of gaining information from prisoners. "Torture and so forth—and I saw the Nazis do this in World War II—gives you bad information because the people will either give you something to make you go away and stop and satisfy you with what you want to hear, rather than really what is true, or they will very courageously die."[31]

The Pentagon Papers

Despite the Vietcong's loss of influence in the South as well as the damage inflicted by the bombing campaign, North Vietnamese leaders steadfastly refused to give ground at the Paris peace talks. By then public opinion in America continued to run overwhelmingly against continuing the war, but Nixon held to his belief that he could bomb the enemy into submission. He said, "I will not be the first president of the United States to lose a war."[32]

In 1971, though, secret facts about the war were revealed, throwing public opinion even more sharply against the president. In June the *New York Times* and *Washington Post* began publishing portions of a seven-thousand-page State Department report that had been leaked to reporters by Daniel Ellsberg, a former State Department official. The report, known as the Pentagon Papers, chronicled the thirty-year history of America's involvement in Vietnam. It indicated that Johnson had escalated the war into Laos as far back as 1964, ordering air strikes

Publication of the secret Pentagon Papers in the largest U.S. magazines and newspapers continued to turn the tide of war against the Nixon administration.

and ground attacks long before Nixon publicly acknowledged attacking Communist positions in Laos in 1971. Other previously unknown missions and incursions by American troops were reported as well. Also, the report suggested that Johnson had made a decision to commit the full might of the American military in Vietnam within the first few months of the conflict, when many U.S. officials believed a diplomatic solution to the crisis still was available.

Nixon reacted sharply to the release of the Pentagon Papers. He insisted that their publication would endanger America's foreign policy, and he asked the two newspapers to stop publishing the report. The *Times* and *Post* refused, but U.S. attorney general John Mitchell won a court order prohibiting publication of the papers. Within days, however, the U.S. Supreme Court ruled that the Nixon administration had no right to tell a newspaper what it could and could not publish. The newspapers resumed publishing the Pentagon Papers, marking a tremendous victory for freedom of the press in the United States.

Breakthrough in Paris

Soon after publication of the Pentagon Papers, President Thieu won re-election in South Vietnam. The United States continued to

Fragging

During the final years of the Vietnam War, some American officers were targeted by their own men. Often those targeted were new officers who had arrived in camp eager to lead missions into the jungle. Many of the enlisted men, seasoned through months of battle, found the new officers incompetent and reckless. By then morale already was low among many of the troops, who wanted nothing more than for the war to be over so they could go home.

In *The Ten Thousand Day War* Michael Maclear quoted Vietnam veteran Mike Beaman: "We used to refuse certain missions because we thought they were brutal. If I didn't want to go in a certain direction, if I felt that we were going to have a confrontation and shoot people for no reason at all, other than to get a body count, I'd say, 'No . . . I'm going this way. You, officer, can go that way, but the other people will follow me.'"

Poor leadership and low morale sometimes led to soldiers victimizing their officers by fragging. This was the practice of rolling a fragmentation grenade (a grenade with a casing that shatters into many destructive pieces when detonated) into the tent of a sleeping officer or other leader. Between 1969 and 1972, 86 officers and noncommissioned officers, including sergeants and corporals, were killed in fragging incidents, while another 714 sustained wounds. In addition some 15 percent of all U.S. casualties in the war were attributed to friendly fire, meaning that the troops were killed or wounded by shots fired from their own ranks. While most of the friendly fire incidents were accidental, military investigators believe some of the shootings were intentional.

Quoted in Michael Maclear, *The Ten Thousand Day War: Vietnam, 1945–1975.* New York: St. Martin's, 1981, p. 271.

support Thieu, even though his status was a major stumbling block in the Paris peace talks. The North Vietnamese refused to deal with Thieu, insisting that he resign and that another leader take control of the government in the South. Nixon and his chief negotiator, national security adviser Henry Kissinger, knew that any president approved by the North Vietnamese would surely be a puppet of the Hanoi regime, so they refused to agree to Thieu's ouster.

The bombing of the North persisted into 1972. Early in the year Nixon traveled to China, becoming the first American president to visit the country since the Communist takeover in 1949. A few months later Nixon visited the Soviet Union. He met personally with leaders of the two countries with the most influence

Le Duc Tho and Henry Kissinger shake hands after both sign a 1973 peace treaty that concluded U.S. involvement in the Vietnam War.

over North Vietnam. In China Nixon found the country's leaders receptive to talks that would end the war.

The Chinese had long been wary of the Soviets. They wanted the United States to remain a presence in South Vietnam to keep the Soviet Union in check. They feared that if the Americans left, the Soviets would dominate Vietnam and establish bases along the Vietnam-

China border. Likewise, Nixon found the Soviets conciliatory as well. By then the Soviets were more concerned with the nuclear arms race against the United States, and they desperately wanted to discuss a treaty that would limit nuclear proliferation. To obtain the treaty, Soviet officials indicated they would press the North Vietnamese to agree to a cease-fire. In May 1972 Nixon announced a new series of bombings in the North as well as the mining of Haiphong harbor in North Vietnam—an action that could endanger Soviet shipping. When the Soviets raised just a token protest about the mining, Nixon knew the pieces had fallen into place to end the war.

Even so, the peace talks would drag on for months. Whenever the North Vietnamese balked and refused to give ground, Nixon ordered a resumption of the bombing. Finally, on October 26, 1972, after a series of intense talks, Kissinger and chief North Vietnamese negotiator Le Duc Tho emerged from a meeting in Paris. Kissinger announced, "We believe peace is at hand."[33]

Chapter Five

The Failure of Vietnamization

The cease-fire that Henry Kissinger and Le Duc Tho negotiated recognized that Vietnam was one country with two governments. President Thieu would remain in power in South Vietnam, and the two sides would work toward a political settlement that would allow the people of Vietnam to decide their future in free elections. All American combat troops would be withdrawn from South Vietnam, and the North Vietnamese would release American prisoners. The defense of South Vietnam would be turned over to the ARVN, but North Vietnamese troops already camped in the South would be permitted to hold their positions. Thieu balked at that condition and at first refused to sign the agreement, but eventually he fell under intense pressure from the United States and agreed to the terms.

President Nixon assured Thieu that he had not abandoned the South, promising that the United States would return should the North Vietnamese violate the terms of the cease-fire and attack the South. Soon, however, Nixon found himself caught up in the Watergate scandal, which led to his resignation in the summer of 1974. Seeing Nixon weakened politically, North Vietnamese leaders started planning an assault on South Vietnam.

When the North Vietnamese army moved into South Vietnam on January 6, 1975, Congress had no stomach for recommitting troops to the Vietnam War. Without U.S. air support, the ARVN was no match for the North Vietnamese army and the Vietcong. The Communists had prepared for a two-year campaign. Instead, their sweep through the South took less than three months.

Discrediting Daniel Ellsberg

Nixon's presidency started unraveling on the night of June 17, 1972, when five burglars were caught inside the office of the

Democratic National Committee in the Watergate hotel and office complex in Washington, D.C. The men were found with electronic eavesdropping equipment; clearly, they intended to set up the equipment and place the office under surveillance. As the Watergate scandal unfolded, it was revealed that operatives working for Nixon's reelection committee had hired the burglars. They had hoped to develop intelligence on the Democrats, especially Nixon's opponent in the fall election, Senator George McGovern of South Dakota.

Eventually, the full breadth of the affair became public. The Watergate burglars were merely one small cog in a widespread campaign intended to guarantee Nixon's reelection in 1972. Part of the plan included sending a team of burglars into the office of the psychiatrist of Daniel Ellsberg, the former State Department official who had leaked the Pentagon Papers. The burglars were planning to use Ellsberg's psychological records to discredit him.

The details of the Watergate scandal were not yet widely known in the fall of 1972, and so Nixon did win re-election, easily sweeping aside McGovern. Shortly after the Watergate break-in, Nixon's press secretary, Ron Ziegler, dismissed the

Duong Van Minh

The last president of South Vietnam, Duong Van Minh, served for less than forty-eight hours before he surrendered the country to the North Vietnamese army. Minh was a former military leader who had long opposed the regime of President Nguyen Van Thieu. At more than 6 feet (1.8m) tall—rare for a Vietnamese—Minh was known as "Big Minh."

Minh was never a hard-line anticommunist and hoped to offer an alternative to the Thieu regime. He briefly had held power in 1963 after the coup against President Ngo Dinh Diem, then fled the country for four years after a new faction of army officers took control of the government. Minh returned to South Vietnam in 1968 and tried to run for president in 1971, but he withdrew from the campaign, claiming U.S. agents had worked against him. After Thieu resigned and fled the country, South Vietnamese government leaders turned to Minh, hoping the Communists would accept him and negotiate favorable terms with him for the South's surrender.

They were wrong. Soon after the surrender, Minh was arrested and imprisoned. He was released in 1983 and permitted to leave the country. Minh went first to France, then moved to the United States. He died in 2001 at the age of eighty-five.

incident as a "third-rate burglary attempt"[34] not worthy of further White House comment.

By 1973, though, Watergate had gained national attention. Congress convened hearings on the scandal, and witnesses testified that Nixon and his aides had resorted to dirty politics in part because they feared that if opponents of the war gained popular support, they would force the White House into accepting a foreign policy favoring North Vietnam. White House counsel John W. Dean III said that Nixon was obsessed with stifling the antiwar protesters. According to Dean, that is why it became so important to discredit Ellsberg. Although Nixon was not in office during the period covered by the Pentagon Papers, he still believed their secrets should remain hidden. He feared that fresh revelations about the war would turn the public further against continuing the fight.

Days after Ellsberg leaked the Pentagon Papers, Nixon had ordered the U.S. Justice Department to charge him with conspiracy, theft, and violations of espionage statutes. The charges were eventually dismissed after evidence of government misconduct—the break-in at his psychiatrist's office—were revealed. Dean later explained:

> I had only a newspaper knowledge of Dan Ellsberg, the man who leaked the Pentagon Papers, a government study of the Vietnam War which showed the government's ineptness, callousness, and deceitfulness in fighting that Asian battle, to the *New York Times*. I knew, as he knew, that the criminal charges the government brought against him were largely fueled by Nixon's pique at his leaking these documents, even though they did not directly affect Nixon.[35]

Digging for the Truth

As journalists, prosecutors, and members of Congress probed for the truth, Nixon dug in and fought back. Much of his time was consumed with fighting the charges and keeping White House records—particularly audiotapes of his Oval Office conversations—out of the hands of prosecutors. The scandal would have a tremendous bearing on American activity in Vietnam.

Years later Kissinger maintained that the Watergate scandal was a decisive factor in the fall of South Vietnam. The president, fighting against congressional inquiries that were digging for the truth about Watergate, was not in a position to ask Congress to send troops back to Southeast Asia. In fact, according to Kissinger, the North Vietnamese were following the progress of the Watergate hearings rather closely themselves. They had come to the astute conclusion that Nixon had been weakened politically and could never muster support in Congress to send ground troops, or even air support, back to South Vietnam. Seeing an opportunity, the Communists started planning to attack the South. Kissinger later wrote:

> After June 1973 I did not believe that the cease-fire would hold. Watergate

Richard Nixon waves from the door of his helicopter after resigning from office due to the Watergate scandal.

was in full swing. We had already acquired intelligence documents in which the North Vietnamese had made the very correct analysis that Nixon would not be in a position to repeat [the bombing of] 1972, because of his domestic difficulties. The congressional agitation to end all military activities in Southeast Asia was already in full force. [36]

Unable to keep the incriminating tapes out of the hands of prosecutors, and facing certain impeachment in Congress, Nixon resigned on August 9, 1974. By then the Communists had built up troops along their border with the South, sending about one hundred thousand soldiers and their equipment down the Ho Chi Minh Trail—which was now a paved highway. Meanwhile, Thieu was losing control of his government. The livelihoods of millions of South Vietnamese, who had worked as maids, cab drivers, shoe shiners, secretaries, and in thousands of other roles, had depended on the American soldiers. Once the Americans left, their incomes ceased to exist, and the South

North Vietnamese soldiers sit aboard a tank during the final campaign against South Vietnam.

Vietnamese economy was on the verge of collapse.

In addition the government in South Vietnam was running out of money. Thieu found it difficult to pay the army, and as a result, morale was low among South Vietnamese soldiers. The leadership of the ARVN was generally regarded as corrupt. Bribery, embezzlement, and outright robbery occurred in the ranks. Some helicopter pilots insisted on bribes simply to evacuate the wounded. At the time, the United States still was supplying the South Vietnamese army with $1 billion a year in aid, but little of this money seemed to filter down to the rank-and-file soldiers.

Beginning of the End

After studying the deployment of South Vietnamese troops, war planners in the North estimated that it would take as long as two years to defeat the South. In actuality, though, the sweep through the South would prove to be a far easier campaign than they expected. The Communists began that campaign with minor skirmishing against South Vietnamese troops in December 1974. This was a diversionary tactic, meant to draw attention away from a major offensive against the province of Phuoc Long and its capital, Phuoc Long City. The city, along the Cambodian border and about 62 miles (100km) west of Saigon, fell on January 6, 1975; of the fifty-four hundred South Vietnamese defenders of the city, fewer than one thousand survived the battle.

Despite the slaughter of the South Vietnamese troops, the United States stayed on the sidelines. Although the new American president, Gerald R. Ford, had made the same pledge of support to Thieu that Nixon had made, he found himself unable to back up his promise. Ford was convinced that with American air support, the South Vietnamese could at least fight the North to a stalemate. In the meantime Ford planned to send diplomats back to Vietnam to negotiate a new cease-fire with the North. He asked Congress to commit another $722 million to the South and to resume air support for the South Vietnamese troops, but Congress refused. Millicent Fenwick, a member of Congress from New Jersey, explained why she was against the spending: "We've sent, so to speak, battleship after battleship, and bomber after bomber, and 500,000 or more men, and billions and billions of dollars. If billions and billions didn't do at a time when we had all our men there, how can $722 million save the day?" [37]

In Vietnam fierce fighting broke out in other provinces and cities. After taking Phuoc Long, the Communists targeted the Central Highlands, where the city of Banmethuot fell under attack. Leading the Communist assault on the South was General Van Tien Dung, who had been a part of the military leadership that defeated the French at Dien Bien Phu. On March 1 he unleashed the attack on Banmethuot, first pummeling the city with artillery and then sending roughly eighty thousand soldiers against a contingent of South Vietnamese defenders of roughly equal size. Yet in defending Banmethuot the South Vietnamese commander, General Pham Van Phu, made a tactical blunder. Because he believed the main assault would occur

Colonel William B. Nolde

Under the truce negotiated in Paris, the Vietnam cease-fire was set to start at 8 A.M. on January 28, 1973, Washington, D.C., time. Eleven hours earlier, at 9 P.M. on January 27, the North Vietnamese launched artillery shells against the city of Anloc near the Cambodian border. Killed in the shelling was Colonel William B. Nolde. He was the last American to die in combat in Vietnam. Four other Americans lost their lives in the week preceding the cease-fire.

Born in Menominee, Michigan, in 1929, Nolde taught military science at Central Michigan University before enlisting in the U.S. Army. He served first in the Korean War and then in Vietnam.

Other Americans lost their lives in Vietnam after the cease-fire took effect, but their deaths were regarded as accidental. Nolde's was the last death attributed to enemy fire. He was the 57,957th casualty of war in Vietnam. Nolde was buried in Arlington National Cemetery on February 5, 1973.

against the nearby city of Pleiku, he had shifted most of his forces to that city, leaving Banmethuot an easy target for the enemy. Dung fed Phu's belief, sending a diversionary force against Pleiku, but the real thrust of the attack was aimed at Banmethuot.

The South Vietnamese soldiers fought hard, and despite Phu's tactical error they held out until March 11, when the city finally fell. Thieu ordered Phu to try to retake the city. Troops were rushed to the Central Highlands and a counteroffensive was launched on March 15, but the South Vietnamese were beleaguered by miscommunications and other errors by the military leadership. Tank and artillery support arrived too late, and the army was plagued by desertions. Many of the defenders had families in Banmethuot

and broke ranks to try to find them. According to General Phillip B. Davidson, who headed U.S. Army intelligence in Vietnam, "While the battle of Phuoc Long marked a major turning point in the Indochina War . . . by demonstrating the impotence of both the ARVN and the United States, it was the ARVN's loss at Banmethuot which marked the beginning of the end for the Republic of Vietnam."[38]

Pleiku, also in the Central Highlands, fell next. Tens of thousands of refugees made their way east from the Central Highlands to the port city of Da Nang, where they hoped to buy passage on ships that would either take them south or even to safe harbors in other countries. Many of the refugees were South Vietnamese soldiers, who had thrown away their weapons, stripped off their uniforms, and joined their families, hoping to find a means to escape. Thousands of refugees were able to escape from Da Nang, but thousands were forced to stay behind. Just north of Da Nang, Hue fell on March 25. Da Nang fell five days later.

The Final Battle

The remaining South Vietnamese troops fell back to mount their final defense of Saigon. The final moment of glory for the ARVN occurred at Xuan Loc, just east of Saigon. Already depleted by casualties and desertions, just five thousand South Vietnamese soldiers remained to defend Xuan Loc against the Communist advance.

Meanwhile, General Dung committed forty thousand North Vietnamese army soldiers to the battle. Fighting broke out on April 9. Despite incurring heavy losses, the South Vietnamese fought hard and killed more than five thousand of the enemy. Miraculously, the defenders held out until April 22, but they finally collapsed under the North's superior numbers and firepower. "In this final epic stand," Davidson commented, "ARVN demonstrated for the last time that, when properly led, it had the 'right stuff.'"[39]

A day after Xuan Loc fell to the North Vietnamese, President Thieu resigned and fled to Taiwan. He was succeeded by Vice

American and Vietnamese evacuees board a helicopter from a rooftop during the fall of Saigon in 1975.

President Tran Van Huong, an aging, nearly blind bureaucrat. Communist leaders sent word to the South that Huong was unacceptable to them. In Saigon, government leaders met to name a new leader whom they believed could negotiate with the Communists once they arrived. They selected Duong Van Minh, a former South Vietnamese army general who had long opposed the Thieu regime.

Panicked South Vietnamese civilians rush aboard one of the final planes out of Saigon as Communist forces advance on the capital.

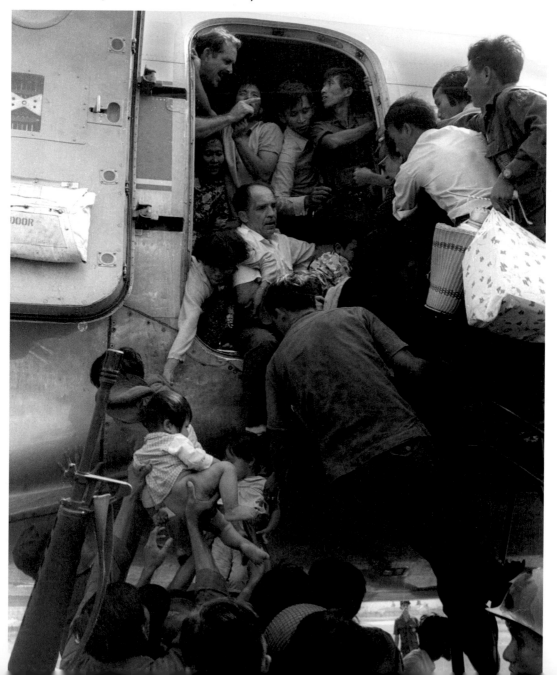

A North Vietnamese army tank penetrates the South Vietnamese presidential palace, the final stronghold of the defeated government.

On April 28 Huong resigned after having been president for only three days, and Minh took his place.

In Saigon, chaos, looting, and a mad rush to escape marked the last days of April 1975. By that point virtually the only way out of the country was by helicopter. In the city the U.S. embassy was still in operation. During the final two days, hundreds of helicopters were dispatched from U.S. aircraft carriers in the South China Sea. They landed on the embassy roof, airlifting embassy staff members, businessmen, journalists, aid workers, and other Americans to safety. At noon on April 29 a Saigon radio station started playing a recording of Bing Crosby's song "White Christmas" every fifteen minutes. Americans knew that was the signal to get out.

They made their way to the embassy roof, where they were evacuated.

Next the American military intended to evacuate as many South Vietnamese citizens as they could. Vietnamese given priority for passage were the government officials, military leaders, and others who had worked closely with the Americans over the years. It was believed that their lives would be in danger once the Communists arrived. South Vietnamese general Tran Van Don, who had been instrumental in selecting Minh as president, recalled the final chaotic hours. He said: "Nobody at the embassy told me what to do—just go to the gate, they said. . . . People were shouting, 'That's General Don— follow him. He can leave. He knows the way out, for sure.'"[40] General Don did make his way onto one of the last helicopters to leave Saigon.

No Resistance

In the United States Americans watched incredible scenes of chaos on their televisions, as thousands of South Vietnamese attempted to flee the North Vietnamese invaders. Many of the South Vietnamese boarded crude and overcrowded boats that sailed into the South China Sea. Thousands of refugees were rescued by U.S. Navy ships cruising just offshore. Meanwhile, at the U.S. embassy in Saigon, cameras caught the final few American helicopters evacuating refugees. Hundreds of refugees were saved in those final few hours, but millions were left behind.

On April 30 North Vietnamese army tanks rolled into Saigon. They entered the city from six directions, finding no resistance at all—Minh had broadcast an order to the remaining South Vietnamese troops to lay down their arms. At 11 A.M. a North Vietnamese tank crashed through the gates of Independence Palace. A lone solider jumped out of the tank and, carrying the flag of the Democratic Republic of Vietnam, rushed into the palace and emerged on an upstairs balcony, where he unfurled the Communist nation's flag. Soon the former South Vietnamese capital would be renamed Ho Chi Minh City.

Inside the palace Colonel Bui Tin, who had fought at Dien Bien Phu, accepted

The *Mayaguez* Incident

The *Mayaguez*, an American commercial ship, was seized by Communist Khmer Rouge gunboats on May 12, 1975, as it sailed in the Gulf of Thailand near the Cambodian coastline. The Khmer Rouge gunboats acted on their own without authority of the Cambodian government.

In Washington President Gerald R. Ford ordered a military response. A boarding party from the *U.S.S. Holt* located the *Mayaguez* anchored off the Cambodian island of Koh Tang, but its thirty-nine-member crew had been removed from the ship. Meanwhile, a force of U.S. Marines, supported by navy ships and aircraft, landed on Koh Tang to search for the crew. The landing party encountered heavy resistance; thirty-eight marines died in the firefight against Khmer Rouge troops. Later that day another American warship, the *U.S.S. Wilson*, found the missing *Mayaguez* crew members; the Khmer Rouge had set them adrift in a fishing boat. In response to the seizure, Ford ordered punitive bombing strikes on Cambodia; bombs hit an oil depot, railroad yard, and airfield on the Cambodian mainland.

President Minh's surrender. The colonel described his thoughts:

> When I saw fear on the faces of Minh and the others present, I said, "The war has ended today, and all Vietnamese are victors. Only the American imperialists are the vanquished. If you still have any feelings for the nation and the people, consider today a happy day." That night, when I sprawled on the lawn of the Independence Palace with members of a communication unit, we all agreed it was the happiest day of our lives because it was a day of complete victory for the nation, because the war ended. [41]

Chapter Six

After the Vietnam War

The Vietnam War had tragic consequences for Vietnam. It is estimated that some 2 million Vietnamese people—an estimated 10 percent of the country's population—lost their lives or were injured during the war. The army of South Vietnam suffered 224,000 killed and 1 million wounded, while the North Vietnamese army reported 1 million dead and 600,000 wounded. In addition countless Vietnamese civilians on both sides of the conflict lost their lives.

North Vietnamese leaders forced their own rigid political culture on the people of the South. They imprisoned thousands of people who had held responsible government or military positions in South Vietnam and shut down many independent businesses. As a result, between 1975 and the early 1990s more than a million Vietnamese fled the country.

Years of warfare also left Vietnam with an infrastructure crushed to rubble by bombing attacks and an environment severely damaged by use of chemical weapons. These problems, coupled with the drain of refugees and economic sanctions imposed by the United States, caused the country's economy to stagnate. Vietnam also had to engage in further warfare. Neighboring Cambodia was overrun by the Communist Khmer Rouge regime that killed more than 1.5 million people—the genocide ended only when the Vietnamese army stepped in and drove the Khmer Rouge out of power. The Vietnamese also had to repel an invasion by China in 1979.

Today, Vietnam is still a Communist country, and its people suffer as a result of government repression. But to Americans communism no longer carries the international threat that seemed to exist in the 1950s and 1960s. The Cold War ended in 1991 with the collapse of the Soviet Union. While some other countries—most notably China—have remained under control of Communist authorities, some perspectives have changed. For example, during the 1990s China was eager to become a trading partner with the United States and has emerged as a significant economic power in Asia. Chinese authorities have hardly wanted to upset their economic plans by exerting Communist ideology onto their free-market neighbors.

And so the Vietnam War turned out to have very little effect on the political situation of the world overall. All those fears expressed by American politicians about the international spread of communism proved to be unfounded. It could be argued that back in 1945, had the United States supported Vietnamese independence and resisted France's desires to recapture its pre–World War II colonies, decades of warfare and bloodshed could have been avoided. But back in 1945 the United States could not bring itself to support a Communist government under any circumstances.

Trouble with Neighbors

After the Vietnam War, Vietnam struggled to establish its new place in Southeast Asia. The country soon found trouble

Bombing and constant warfare left much of Vietnam in ruin by the time the Communist takeover was complete.

brewing on its western border with Cambodia as well as on its northern border with China.

In Cambodia the Khmer Rouge seized power in 1975. For the next four years the regime's leader, Pol Pot, would undertake a bizarre scheme to turn the country into a society of communal farms. Hundreds of thousands of citizens were driven out of their homes and forced to live on small farms in the countryside. Anybody suspected of dissent was murdered. Hun-

Khmer Rouge guerillas rest briefly in the Chardanrom mountains. The regime murdered 1 million civilians during the span of its power in Cambodia.

Nguyen Cao Ky

Following the fall of Saigon in 1975, thousands of South Vietnamese citizens fled to the United States, where they started new lives. One Vietnamese man who made the transition was Nguyen Cao Ky, who served as commander of the South Vietnamese air force and also as prime minister and vice president.

Ky rose to power in the government in the years following the coup that toppled President Ngo Dinh Diem. From the time of the coup in 1963 until the election of Nguyen Van Thieu in 1967, the country was led by a series of unstable military leaders. Ky helped stabilize the country and enabled Thieu to govern effectively. Many insiders believed Ky held the real power in the South Vietnam government.

After fleeing Vietnam in 1975, Ky settled in California, where he opened a grocery store. At the age of seventy-four, Ky returned to Vietnam in 2004 for a visit, spending the week sightseeing and visiting old friends. Ky told a reporter that the Communist leaders of the country realize it is important for American companies to invest in Vietnam. "Younger men, in their 50s and 60s, are in charge of Hanoi," he said. "They know they have to get on with America."

Quoted in Jane Perlez, "After Decades, Saigon Figure Visits Vietnam with U.S. Nod," *New York Times*, January 26, 2004, p. A-4.

dreds of thousands also died from starvation. By 1979 it is believed that more than 1 million Cambodians died under the regime of the Khmer Rouge. When the regime started targeting Vietnamese living in Cambodia and also making incursions across the border into Vietnam, the Vietnamese military invaded Cambodia to oust the Khmer Rouge. Pol Pot and the other leaders of the movement were chased into the jungle, where they hid for years. In the meantime a United Nations peacekeeping force stepped in to stabilize the country, and eventually a representative democracy emerged there. Occasional fighting still breaks out in Cambodia,

however, and its government is considered one of the most corrupt in the world.

As for Laos, in 1975 the Vietnamese-backed Pathet Lao signed a treaty with the government of Laos giving the Communist organization tremendous influence over the country. The Pathet Lao ran the government of Laos until 1990; a 1976 treaty allowed Vietnam to house a large contingent of troops in Laos, essentially making the smaller country a Vietnamese colony. Vietnam eventually withdrew its troops and the Pathet Lao disbanded, but a Communist government continues to administer the country. Laos remains a poor country—its 2006 gross domestic product per capita, a measure of each worker's share in the national income, was just $2,100.

Vietnam has maintained a sometimes testy relationship with China, its one-time ally. In 1979 that relationship disintegrated. Armies of the two countries clashed after Vietnam signed a friendship pact with the Soviet Union and started driving out Chinese citizens who had settled in the North. Chinese military commanders, believing the Vietnamese army had been weakened because it had committed some one hundred thousand troops to the conflict against the Khmer Rouge, sent eighty thousand soldiers across the border. Entering Vietnam on February 17, the Chinese soldiers encountered heavy resistance, though, and got no further than the city of Lang Son, about 25 miles (40km) south of the border. On March 16, the Chinese withdrew from the country.

After the skirmishes in 1979 the Vietnamese and Chinese were slow to patch up their differences. In 1991 the two countries agreed to resume trade. They further expanded their economic ties to one another in 2005, when they permitted Vietnamese and Chinese businesses to sign deals with one another worth more than $1 billion. Still, the Vietnamese watch China carefully. The two countries each lays claim to the oil-rich Spratly Islands in the South China Sea. Both countries maintain military outposts on the islands. Vietnam and China agreed in 2002 to work toward a resolution of the issue, but by 2007 no agreement had been reached.

Rebuilding Their Country

While Vietnam's leaders struggled with neighbors in Southeast Asia, they also found themselves with the huge task of rebuilding their country. Much of Vietnam's countryside has been decimated by years of warfare—jungles and agricultural lands were burned by napalm (a substance used in flamethrowers and fire bombs) and defoliated by Agent Orange. Today, young children still are born in Vietnam with birth defects caused by the lingering effects of Agent Orange. The chemicals used copiously during the Vietnam War have also contributed to higher-than-normal rates of cancer and other illnesses.

In the years following the war, the Vietnamese were in need of new roads, utilities, homes, fuel, and most of the other necessities of life. When journalist Peter T. White visited Hanoi in 1989, he found little progress had been made in the fourteen years since the North's victory. White found that the Vietnamese economy lacked the ability to support the nation's people. "Officially, per capita income is equivalent to just over a hundred U.S. dollars a year," he said. "To make ends meet, a doctor in charge of a hospital has had to be a janitor at night. A distinguished general in retirement must depend on his wife selling cigarettes in the street; she walks two miles a day so she won't have to lose face with the neighbors."[42]

For the Vietnamese, things would get even worse economically. After the end of the war, the Vietnamese government had relied on the Soviet Union for economic aid. This aid dried up as the Soviet Union collapsed in the late 1980s, sending Vietnam's economy further into a tailspin. Ironically, a leading factor in the collapse of the Soviet Union was the disastrous decision by Soviet leaders to wage war in Afghanistan. The war—often called "Russia's Vietnam"—severely hobbled the Communist country and called into question the ability of the Soviet army to win a war.

Following the Soviet collapse, the United States and Vietnam took their first tentative steps toward reconciliation. At the end of the Vietnam War, the United States had maintained a trade embargo against Vietnam, making it illegal for American companies to do business in the Asian country. But in 1993 President Bill Clinton started removing the trade barriers to Vietnam, permitting American corporations to invest in the country. The change in policy also permitted Americans to visit the country. In 1995 Vietnam established an embassy in Washington, D.C. In 2004 journalist David Lamb, who had covered the Vietnam War in the 1960s and 1970s,

A Vietnamese woman strolls past an American billboard in Vietnam, exactly one year after President Bill Clinton removed the country's economic trade embargo.

returned to Southeast Asia and visited Hanoi. In describing the city, Lamb said it appeared that the Vietnamese had worked hard to put the war behind them:

By breakfast time the sidewalks have been claimed by women in conical hats hawking vegetables and flowers, by vendors selling 20-cent bowls of lemon-grass-flavored chicken noodle soup known as pho ga—Hanoians will tell you their pho and bia (beer) are far superior to what is produced in Ho Chi Minh City—and by gaggles of motor scooters with nowhere else to park. Everyone is busy: sewing, welding, jackhammering, lugging, selling, cooking, repairing, sawing, building.

This energetic, industrious Hanoi is the only one I have known. It was difficult to imagine what people here told me: That less than 20 years ago, Hanoi was a miserable, dispirited place, a city where children gathered at night to study under outdoor gas lamps and adults shuffled the streets with slumped shoulders and a look of grim preoccupation. The euphoria of victory had been brief. In many ways, winning the peace has proved as difficult as waging the war. [43]

Despite some improvements Vietnam is still a Communist country, and in many ways, its people are forced to live under the repression that has characterized Communist governments elsewhere. In the Soviet Union before its collapse and today in China, Cuba, and other Communist countries, freedom of expression is stifled. Dissent is seldom tolerated. Electoral power is not held by the people. Today in Vietnam, the government maintains tight control over the country's newspapers, radio stations, and television stations. Vietnamese citizens who have posted pro-democracy messages on the Internet have been arrested.

In 2007 Vietnamese prime minister Nguyen Tan Dung took the unprecedented action of hosting a chat session with his country's Internet users. About twenty thousand Vietnamese citizens sent messages to Dung during the two-hour chat session. Some of the Internet users questioned the lack of press freedom in Vietnam, while others complained about the government's seizure of private farmland. Dung fielded as many questions as he could during the online chat, generally defending the government's activities. Later some citizens of the country praised the prime minister for the rare opportunity he gave them to question the government. Hanoi taxi driver Nguyen Trung Van told a reporter: "I don't know whether the issues we raised to our leaders will be addressed or not. But this is a good start because we need a channel to communicate with our leaders." [44]

Dung, who joined the Vietcong in 1962 at the age of twelve, acknowledged during the online chat that he had sent his son to college in the United States. "We do not hate the American people," [45] he insisted.

Effect in the United States

In the United States the Vietnam War had a major effect on the U.S. military. In 1973,

Prime Minister Dung fields personal and political questions during a historic online chat with the nation of Vietnam.

with no more need to conscript soldiers, President Nixon ended the draft. Since then the U.S. military has been an all-volunteer force, relying on people who enlist because they want to serve. The number of American soldiers has grown significantly smaller since Vietnam, in part because the end of the Cold War made a large standing army unnecessary, and in part because new technologies have been developed to do jobs that soldiers once did.

It took more than a decade for the U.S. military to recover from the defeat in Viet-

nam. Most experts agree, however, that in many ways the modern all-volunteer army is more effective and has higher morale than the larger Vietnam-era forces. Soldiers today enlist for longer tours of duty, so they are better trained than were the draftees of the 1960s and early 1970s. The success of the all-volunteer army was shown in the 1991 Gulf War and again in the 2003 invasion of Iraq.

What has also changed since Vietnam, however, is a willingness of the American people to suffer casualties in a protracted ground war. During the 1980s and 1990s numerous military and civilian leaders established guidelines that should be followed before the U.S. would commit to military action. One of the most famous of these, as elaborated by General Colin Powell at the end of the 1991 Gulf War, is known as the Powell Doctrine. Powell had served in Vietnam as a major and stayed in the military through the transition to an all-volunteer force. According to the Powell Doctrine, the United States would only commit forces in the case of a vital threat to national security, and only after all other means to find a peaceful solution had been exhausted. The United States would rely on overwhelming force to win a clear military victory, then retire from the battlefield without becoming involved in a Vietnam-style entanglement. In a 1992 essay published in the journal *Foreign Affairs*, Powell explained:

> We owe it to the men and women who go in harm's way to make sure that . . . their lives are not squandered for unclear purposes.
>
> We must not, for example, send military forces into a crisis with an unclear mission they cannot accomplish—such as we did when we sent the U.S. Marines into Lebanon in 1983. We inserted those proud warriors into the middle of a five-faction civil war complete with terrorists, hostage-takers, and a dozen spies in every camp, and said, "Gentlemen, be a buffer." The results were 241 Marines and Navy personnel killed and a U.S. withdrawal from the troubled area. [46]

Throughout the 1990s U.S. leaders followed this policy. In 1994 President Bill Clinton refused to send U.S. soldiers to intervene in Rwanda, where between 800,000 and 1 million people were massacred in a systematic program of genocide. In 1999 Clinton ruled out the intervention of U.S. ground troops in Kosovo, where a bloody civil war was being waged, although he did authorize high-altitude bombing and cruise missile strikes.

Forgotten Lessons

By 2003, however, George W. Bush had become president and the United States found itself facing a new enemy: Islamic fundamentalists who threatened to wage war against American interests using terrorist tactics. Bush and his advisers feared that Iraqi dictator Saddam Hussein possessed weapons of mass destruction and that he would sell them to the terrorists. In March 2003 the U.S. military invaded Iraq.

Like Vietnam, the Iraq War turned into a protracted military campaign that eventually lost the support of most Americans. At the outset, Bush had received considerable support in Congress and from the American people when he decided to invade Iraq. American troops easily swept aside the Iraqi military, captured Saddam, and installed a democratic government. But the situation quickly deteriorated into a civil war as opposing religious factions battled for control of the country. Each day brought new reports of dozens, or even hundreds, of Iraqis killed in terrorist attacks and infighting among warring factions. American troops were targeted as well, as the insurgents wanted them out of the country.

Bush refused to pull out the troops because he did not want to leave before the country was stabilized. As a result, the war dragged on, and by early 2007, more than thirty-five hundred Americans had lost their lives in the conflict. Most of them died in sniper attacks or by falling victim to roadside bombs that exploded as their vehicles drove by—tactics not unlike those practiced forty years ago by the Vietcong. Writing in *U.S. News & World Report*, journalist Julian E. Barnes said: "One can safely say that Iraq is not the kind of war for which the . . . U.S. Army spent decades preparing. In fact, Iraq is the kind of fight that, after Vietnam, the Army hoped to avoid. It is a messy war in an urban landscape against multiple insurgencies, a powder keg of ethnic tensions that the United States does not completely understand." [47]

In addition, just as the atrocities of My Lai and the street executions of Vietcong guerillas horrified Americans in the 1960s, similar stories in Iraq added to the public's furor over the war. In late 2005 a squad of U.S. Marines was accused of murdering twenty-four unarmed Iraqi citizens in

Vietnam Veterans Memorial

More than 3 million people a year visit the Vietnam Veterans Memorial in Washington, D.C., which was dedicated in 1982. The main feature of the memorial is a 246-foot black granite wall (75m) in which the names of nearly sixty thousand men and women who either died in Vietnam or remain missing in action have been etched. Standing near the wall is another well-known feature, a statue depicting three weary American servicemen as they would have appeared during the height of the conflict. The statue is known as *The Three Soldiers.*

The wall was designed by Maya Ying Lin, a Chinese American woman who at the time was an architecture student at Yale University. She submitted the design as part of an open competition and was declared the winner by the committee that had been named to select a design for the memorial. At the time, the selection was controversial. Critics complained that a black wall would not adequately demonstrate the drama of the war. To respond to those critics, the selection committee agreed to include *The Three Soldiers* in the memorial, and sculptor Frederick Hart was commissioned to provide the work of art. Racism also found its way into the controversy, as some critics suggested that a design submitted by a woman of Asian ethnicity was inappropriate because the war had pitted Asians against Americans. But the committee dismissed such criticisms and stuck with Lin's design for the memorial.

the town of Haditha, conjuring up memories of My Lai. By this time shocking photographs and reports emerged about inhumane conditions at Abu Ghraib, a U.S. military prison in Iraq. When Congress convened hearings into the abuse of prisoners at Abu Ghraib, a stunned Senator John McCain—who had been tortured for six years as a prisoner in North Vietnam—said: "I have seen a lot of people die. I've seen a lot of terrible things in my life. But to see it done by Americans to human

U.S. troops patrol the site of a suicide bombing in Iraq. Many comparisons have been drawn between the two American conflicts.

Pol Pot

During the 1970s Pol Pot emerged as one of history's most notorious dictators. Under his regime, known as the Khmer Rouge, some 1.5 million Cambodians were murdered or died from starvation as Pol Pot tried to forge a rural society of communal farms.

Born Saloth Sar in Kompong Thom, Cambodia, in 1928, he traveled to France after World War II, where he joined the French Communist Party. Sar returned to Cambodia in 1953, determined to spread communism to the country. Back in Cambodia he took the name Pol Pot, which means "the original Cambodian." By 1966 he had emerged as the leader of the Khmer Rouge, and nine years later he took control of the government.

After his ouster he remained committed to his cause to the end and was never brought to justice. Pol Pot remained in hiding deep in the jungles of Thailand and Cambodia, although he also was reported to be living in China. In 1998 the remnants of the Khmer Rouge leadership agreed to turn Pol Pot over for trial by an international tribunal. He died the night of April 15, 1998, while waiting to be taken into custody. Shortly before his death Pol Pot is reported to have said, "My conscience is clear."

Quoted in "Pol Pot: Life of a Tyrant," BBC News, April 14, 2000. http://news.bbc.co.uk/1/hi/world/asia-pacific/78988.stm.

beings is what's so appalling. It's so outrageous, I can't describe it."[48]

Many people have compared the war in Iraq to the Vietnam War, noting that the Bush administration ordered the invasion of Iraq without having a clear strategy in place to win the peace. They also argued that U.S. leaders did not understand their enemy and had therefore underestimated the willingness of Iraqi insurgents to keep fighting. These are the most important lessons that can be learned from the Vietnam War, and future American leaders would do well to keep them in mind.

Notes

Introduction: The Vietnam War

1. Quoted in American Presidency Project, University of California Santa Barbara, "Lyndon Johnson, Remarks to the International Platform Association upon Receiving the Association's Annual Award," August 3, 1965. www.presidency.ucsb.edu/ws/index.php?pid=27126.

2. Townsend Hoopes, "Legacy of the Cold War in Indochina," *Foreign Affairs*, July 1970, p. 609.

Chapter One: Elusive Independence

3. Quoted in Marilyn B. Young, *The Vietnam Wars*. New York: Harper-Perennial, 1991, p. 3.

4. Quoted in Young, *The Vietnam Wars*, pp. 7–8.

5. Quoted in *The American Experience*, PBS, "Vietnam Online." www.pbs.org/wgbh/amex/vietnam/series/pt_01.html.

6. Quoted in *The American Experience*, PBS, "Vietnam Online." www.pbs.org/wgbh/amex/vietnam/series/pt_01.html.

7. Quoted in *The American Experience*, PBS, "Vietnam Online." www.pbs.org/wgbh/amex/vietnam/series/pt_01.html.

Chapter Two: Escalation

8. Quoted in *The American Experience*, PBS, "Vietnam Online."

9. Quoted in Stanley Karnow, *Vietnam: A History*. New York: Penguin, 1997, p. 429.

10. Quoted in *The American Experience*, PBS, "Vietnam Online."

11. Quoted in Young, *The Vietnam Wars*, p 144.

12. Quoted in *The American Experience*, PBS, "Vietnam Online."

13. Quoted in Young, *The Vietnam Wars*, p. 167.

14. Quoted in Young, *The Vietnam Wars*, p. 210.

15. Quoted in Young, *The Vietnam Wars*, p. 215.

16. Quoted in *The American Experience*, PBS, "Vietnam Online."

17. Quoted in Young, *The Vietnam Wars*, p. 217.

Chapter Three: Struggle in the United States

18. Quoted in Southern Methodist University, "Walter Cronkite's 'We Are Mired in Stalemate' Broadcast," February 27, 1969. http://faculty.smu.edu/dsimon/Change%20—Cronkite.html.

19. Quoted in Don Oberdorfer, "Tet: Who Won?" *Smithsonian*, November 2004, p. 117.

20. Martin Luther King Jr., "This Madness Must Cease," Centre for Research of Globalization. www.globalresearch.ca/index.php?context=viewArticle&code=%20KI20070115&articleId=4460.

21. Abbie Hoffman, *Soon to Be a Major Motion Picture*. New York: Berkley, 1982, p. 151.

22. Quoted in Michael Bilton and Kevin Sim, *Four Hours in My Lai*. New York: Viking Penguin, 1992, p. 219.

23. Quoted in Michael Maclear, *The Ten Thousand Day War: Vietnam, 1945–1975*. New York: St. Martin's, 1981, p. 275.

24. John McCain and Mark Salter, *Faith of My Fathers: A Family Memoir*. New York: Random House, 1999, pp. 242–43.

25. McCain and Salter, *Faith of My Fathers*, p. 345.

Chapter Four: "Peace Is at Hand"

26. Quoted in Karnow, *Vietnam*, p. 597.

27. Quoted in Young, *The Vietnam Wars*, p. 238.

28. David Wise and Thomas B. Ross, *The Invisible Government: The CIA and U.S. Intelligence*. New York: Vintage, 1974, p. 148.

29. Quoted in Young, *The Vietnam Wars*, p. 271.

30. Quoted in Maclear, *The Ten Thousand Day War*, p. 260.

31. Quoted in Maclear, *The Ten Thousand Day War*, pp. 260–61.

32. Quoted in Karnow, *Vietnam*, p. 592.

33. Quoted in *The American Experience*, PBS, "Vietnam Online."

Chapter Five: The Failure of Vietnamization

34. Quoted in Bob Woodward and Carl Bernstein, *All the President's Men*. New York: Warner, 1975, p. 26.

35. John W. Dean III, *Lost Honor*. Los Angeles: Stratford, 1982, p. 61.

36. Quoted in *The American Experience*, PBS, "Vietnam Online."

37. Quoted in *The American Experience*, PBS, "Vietnam Online."

38. Phillip B. Davidson, *Vietnam at War: The History, 1946–1975*. Novato, CA: Presidio, 1988, p. 769.

39. Davidson, *Vietnam at War*, p. 790.

40. Quoted in Maclear, *The Ten Thousand Day War*, p 342.

41. Quoted in *The American Experience*, PBS, "Vietnam Online."

Chapter Six: After the Vietnam War

42. Peter T. White, "Vietnam: Hard Road to Peace," *National Geographic*, November 1989, p. 570.

43. David Lamb, "Hanoi: Shedding the Ghosts of War," *National Geographic*, May 2004, p. 80.

44. Quoted in Margie Mason, Associated Press, "Vietnam's Leader Goes to

the People—Online," *Philadelphia Inquirer*, February 10, 2007, p. A-4.

45. Quoted in Mason, "Vietnam's Leader Goes to the People—Online," p. A-4.

46. Colin Powell, "US Forces: The Challenges Ahead." *Foreign Affairs*, Winter 1992–1993, pp. 32–45.

47. Julian E. Barnes, "Hard-Learned Lessons," *U.S. News & World Report*, March 27, 2006, p. 42.

48. Quoted in Sheryl Gay Stolberg, "Prisoner Abuse Scandal Puts McCain in Spotlight Once Again," *New York Times*, May 10, 2004, p. A-19.

For Further Reading

Books

Philip Caputo, *10,000 Days of Thunder: A History of the Vietnam War*. New York: Atheneum, 2005. This award-winning book for young readers provides background history on communism and the origins of the war, with easy-to-digest information about American involvement.

W.D. Ehrhart, *Vietnam-Perkasie: A Combat Marine's Memoir*. New York: Zebra, 1983. Bill Ehrhart's autobiography recounts his experiences in Vietnam, including his participation in the Battle of Hue, and the difficulty he had readjusting to life in America.

Mitchell K. Hall, *The Vietnam War*. 2nd ed. New York: Longman, 2007. In addition to a brief history of the war, this book includes more than thirty pages of important documents from the period.

Peter Lowe, ed., *The Vietnam War*. New York: St. Martin's, 1999. The essays in this collection discuss the role of the United States, Soviet Union, China, and other players in the Vietnam War.

Tamara L. Roleff, ed., *The Vietnam War*. San Diego: Greenhaven, 2002. Many aspects of the war are covered in articles and essays written by draft evaders, veterans, members of the Vietcong, prisoners of war, and a survivor of the My Lai massacre.

Robert Russell, *Leaders and Generals*. San Diego: Lucent, 2001. The book chronicles the lives and decisions made by six Vietnam War–era leaders, including Ho Chi Minh, Ngo Dinh Diem, Lyndon B. Johnson, William Westmoreland, Richard Nixon, and Henry Kissinger.

Josepha Sherman, *The Cold War*. Minneapolis: Lerner, 2004. The decades-long Cold War between the United States and Soviet Union is discussed; the book covers the Korean and Vietnam wars, Cuban missile crisis, Soviet invasion of Afghanistan, and collapse of the Soviet Union.

Diane Yancey, *Life of an American Soldier*. San Diego: Lucent, 2001. The book focuses on the plight of the individual soldiers who fought in Vietnam, showing how they were trained, how they existed, the dangers they faced on their missions, and the problems they faced when they returned home.

Periodicals

Don Oberdorfer, "Tet: Who Won?," *Smithsonian*, November 2004.

Amanda Spake, "The Healing Process Is Far from Done," *U.S. News & World Report*, May 1, 2000.

Peter T. White, "Vietnam: Hard Road to Peace," *National Geographic*, November 1989.

Video

Vietnam, A Television History. In DVD format, produced by television station WGBH of Boston, Massachusetts, 1983.

Internet Sources

The American Experience, PBS, "Vietnam Online." www.pbs.org/wgbh/amex/vietnam.

U.S. State Department's Bureau of East Asian and Pacific Affairs, "Background Note: Vietnam." www.state.gov/r/pa/ei/bgn/4130.htm.

Web Sites

Embassy of Vietnam (www.vietnam embassy-usa.org). Vietnam established an embassy in Washington, D.C., in 1995; visitors to the embassy's Web site can read news about the country and learn about Vietnamese culture. The site includes twenty-six lessons in the Vietnamese language. The first lesson is how to say "hello," "xin cháo."

Lyndon B. Johnson (www.lbjlib.utexas.edu). The Web site maintained by the Lyndon Baines Johnson Library and Museum at the University of Texas in Austin includes many online resources, including copies of speeches given by Johnson, an archive of photographs, images from the president's daily diary, and audio and video clips of the former president.

Vietnam Veteran Bill Ehrhart (www.wd ehrhart.com). Students can read several poems written by Vietnam veteran Bill Ehrhart. The site also includes Ehrhart's biography and links to other sites maintained by Vietnam veterans who also have written about their experiences in the war.

Index

A
Abu Ghraib, 90–91
Adams, Eddie, 38
Agent Orange, 52
Antiwar protests, 40–41, 43–46, 49
Army of the Republic of Vietnam
    (ARVN), 32, 73
    defense of South Vietnam, 68
August Revolution (1945), 15–16

B
Ball, George, 29
Bao Dai, 18
Barnes, Julian E., 89
Beaman, Mike, 65
Buddhists, 22–23
Bui Tin. *See* Tin, Bui
Bush, George W., 88, 89

C
Calley, William, 46, 48, 49
Cambodia
    expansion of war into, 55, 58–60
    Khmer Rouge seizes power, 82–83
Cantero, George, 58
Central Intelligence Agency (CIA),
    Phoenix Program and, 63

Chiang Kai-shek, 11, 17
    defeat of, 18
Chicago Seven, 46
Chieu, Pham Xuan, 34
China, Peoples' Republic of, 81
    Nixon's visit to, 65–66
    Vietnam's relationship with, 84
Clinton, Bill, 85, 88
Colby, William, 63
Cold War, 10–11, 80
Conein, Lucien, 25
Cronkite, Walter, 40

D
Daley, Richard, 45
Davidson, Phillip B., 74
Dean, John W., III, 70
Deer Mission, 14
Democratic National Convention
    (1968), 40–41, 45–46
Diem, Ngo Dinh, 20, 21
    coup against, 23–25
Dien Bien Phu, 19
Domino theory, 11
Don, Tran Van, 77–78
Draft, 43, 44
Draft resistance, 31–32
Dung, Nguyen Tan, 86

Dung, Van Tien, 73, 74
Duong Van Minh. *See* Minh, Duong
	Van

E
Ehrhart, Bill, 32
Eisenhower, Dwight D., 20–21, 57
Ellsberg, Daniel, 64
	attempt to discredit, 68–70

F
Fenwick, Millicent, 73
First Indochina War, 17–19
Ford, Gerald R., 73
Foreign Affairs (journal), 88
Fragging, 65

G
Geneva Conventions, 53
Gulf of Tonkin Resolution (1964), 26, 43

H
Haldeman, Bob, 57
Harrington, Myron, 38
Hersh, Seymour, 48
Ho Chi Minh (Nguyen That Thanh),
	13, 14
	calls for Vietnam's independence,
		15–16
	death of, 57–58
	negotiates peace agreement with
		France, 20

Ho Chi Minh Trail, 21, 22, 30–31
	U.S. bombing of, 29
Hoffman, Abbie, 46
Hoopes, Townsend, 12
Hope, Bob, 62
Hue (South Vietnam), 36
Humphrey, Hubert, 35, 45, 46, 56
Huong, Tran Van, 76, 77
Hussein, Saddam, 88

I
Iraq War (2003–), 88–90

J
Johnson, Lyndon B.
	announces will not seek reelection,
		39
	Gulf of Tonkin incident and, 26
	orders Operation Rolling Thunder,
		29
	on reason for U.S. action in Vietnam,
		11

K
Karnow, Stanley, 20
Kennedy, John F., issue ultimatum to
	Diem, 25
Kennedy, Robert F., 45
Kent State Massacre (1970), 50–51
Khe Sahn (South Vietnam), 35–36
Khmer Rouge, 60, 82
King, Martin Luther, Jr., 43–44

Kissinger, Henry, 65, 67, 70–71
Korean War, 11, 18
Ky, Nguyen Cao, 83

L
Lamb, David, 85–86
Laos
   after Vietnam War, 83–84
   expansion of war into, 55, 58, 60
Le Duc Tho. *See* Tho, Le Duc
Lodge, Henry Cabot, 25
Lenin, Vladimir, 14–15
Lin, Maya Ying, 89
Loan, Nguyen Ngoc, 38

M
Maclear, Michael, 65
Maddox (U.S. Navy destroyer), 25
Madman Theory, 57
Mao Tse-tung, 11
   defeats nationalist Chinese, 18
Mayaguez incident (1975), 78
McCain, John, 53–54, 90–91
McCarthy, Eugene, 45
McGovern, George, 69
Minh, Duong Van, 69, 76
Mitchell, John, 64
My Lai Massacre, 46–48

N
National Liberation Front. See Vietcong
New York Times (newspaper), 64

Ngo Dinh Diem. *See* Diem, Ngo Dinh
Ngo Dinh Nhu. *See* Nhu, Ngo Dinh
Nguyen Cao Ky. *See* Ky, Nguyen Cao
Nguyen Ngoc Loan. *See* Loan, Nguyen
   Ngoc
Nguyen Tan Dung. *See* Dung, Nguyen
   Tan
Nguyen That Thanh. *See* Ho Chi Minh
Nguyen Van Thieu. *See* Thieu, Nguyen
   Van
Nhu, Madame, 24
Nhu, Ngo Dinh, 21
Nixon, Richard M., 46, 48, 63
   China trip of, 65–66
   Madman Theory of, 57
   orders stepped-up bombing of
      North, 55
   resignation of, 71
   urges South Vietnam not to negotiate
      peace, 56–57
   Watergate scandal and, 69
Nolde, William B., 74
North Vietnam, 27

O
Operation Rolling Thunder, 29–31
Osborne, Barton, 63

P
Pathet Lao, 60, 83
Peace talks, 67
Pentagon Papers, 63–64
Pham Van Dong, 17

Pham Van Phu, 73–74
Phoenix Program, 63
Phu, Pham Van, 73–74
Piroth, Charles, 20
Pol Pot, 82, 83, 91
Post-traumatic stress disorder, 52
Potter, Paul, 45
Powell, Colin, 88
Powell Doctrine, 88
Prisoners of war (POWs), 52–54

Q
Quang Tri (South Vietnam), 61, 63

R
Ridenhour, Ronald, 47–48
Ross, Thomas B., 60
Rusk, Dean, 18

S
Safer, Morley, 32
Selective Service Commission, 43
Shaplen, Robert, 38–39
Sihanouck, Norodom, 59
Soviet Union
   collapse of, 85
   Nixon's visit to, 65, 67
Students for a Democratic Society, 45

T
Teach-ins, 43
The Ten Thousand Day War (Maclear), 65

Tet Offensive (1968), 34, 35–39, 55
Thieu, Nguyen Van, 35, 56–57, 64–65,
   68, 71
   resignation of, 75
Tho, Le Duc, 67
Thompson, Hugh, Jr., 46–47
Tin, Bui, 78–79
Tran Van Huong. *See* Huong, Tran Van
Tran Van Don. *See* Don, Tran Van
Truman, Harry, 16
Trung Nhi, 13
Trung Trac, 13
Tse-tung, Mao. *See* Mao Tse-tung
Turner Joy (U.S. Navy destroyer),
   25–26
Twenty-sixth Amendment, 49

U
Udall, Morris, 48
United States
   aids French in Vietnam, 18
   legacy of war in, 86–88
   opposition to war in, 40, 49
   support of South Vietnamese Army
      by, 73
United States (1964–1975), bombing of
   North Vietnam by, 27
U.S. News and World Report (magazine),
   89

V
Van Tien Dung. *See* Dung, Van Tien
Veterans, problems facing on return to
   U.S., 51–52

Viet Minh, 14
  August 1945 revolution and, 15–16
  in First Indochina War, 17–18
Vietcong (National Liberation Front),
  21
  Army of South Vietnam vs., 32–33
  peasants join ranks of, 32
Vietnam, 12
  Communism introduced to, 14–15
  drugs in, 58
  first U.S. ground troops arrive in,
    31
  French invasion of, 13–14
  Nationalist Chinese invade, 17
  rebuilding of, 84–86
Vietnam: A History (Karnow), 20
Vietnam Veterans Memorial, 89
Vietnam War (1964–1975)

expands to Laos and Cambodia, 55
final battle of, 75–78
first battle of, 27–28
Vietnamese casualties in, 80
Vietnamization, 60–61, 63

W
Walton, George, 49
Washington Post (newspaper), 64
Watergate scandal, 68, 69
Westmoreland, William C., 34, 35
White, Peter T., 84
Wise, David, 60

Z
Ziegler, Ron, 69–70

Picture Credits

About the Author

Hal Marcovitz is a former newspaper reporter who has written nearly one hundred books for young readers. He lives in Chalfont, Pennsylvania, with his wife, Gail, and daughters Michelle and Ashley.